Fr. Joseph Bittle

AT THE LAST TRUMPET

At the Last Trumpet

Jesus Christ and the End of Time

WILLIAM BARCLAY

Westminster John Knox Press
Louisville, Kentucky

Book design by Sharon Adams
Cover design by Jennifer Cox
Cover photograph © 1998 PhotoDisc, Inc.

First edition
Published by Westminster John Knox Press
Louisville, Kentucky

This book is printed on acid-free paper that meets the
American National Standards Institute Z39.48 standard. ∞

PRINTED IN THE UNITED STATES OF AMERICA
98 99 00 01 02 03 04 05 06 07 — 10 9 8 7 6 5 4 3 2 1

Library of Congress Cataloging-in-Publication Data

Barclay, William, 1907–1978.
    At the last trumpet : Jesus Christ and the end of time / William
Barclay. — 1st ed.
            p.   cm.
    A collection of various writings by the author which were
originally published in The daily study Bible series.
    Includes index.
    ISBN 0-664-25806-9 (alk. paper)
    1. Jesus Christ—Teachings.   2. Eschatology—Biblical teaching.
I. Title.
BS2417.E7B37   1998
236'.9—dc21   98-37925

Contents

Introduction

"For you know neither the day nor the hour."

The much acclaimed and widely popular Daily Study Bible—New Testament was the *magnum opus* of William Barclay. In these volumes, Barclay exposited the scriptures with vivid images that allowed the New Testament to come alive for every reader. Though written decades ago, the Daily Study Bible continues to speak to each generation, and to open up the rich message of God's love and forgiveness found in the New Testament. Within his Daily Study Bible, Barclay was able to comment, not only on that message of God's love, but on other subjects too.

Unfortunately, we do not have a volume with all of Barclay's writings on the subject of the end of time. In this work, an effort has been made to go back into the Daily Study Bible and collect Barclay's most significant insights on the last days. Every effort has been made to glean his best work on the subject, without repeating his thoughts. We are lucky, for Barclay lays out his scheme for what the end of time will be like several times in his introductions to key chapters, or within his discussion of the prominent metaphors. In a nutshell, here is what William Barclay had to say about the subject.

The New Testament was written against the backdrop of Jewish expectations for a Messiah, Jewish apocalyptic understandings about how the Jewish nation would be restored, and an infant Christian church's explanation of an unfulfilled expectation of the soon return of Jesus Christ. Borrowing heavily from the writings of the Old Testament and the time between the Testaments, as well as using references to current events, the writers of the New Testament lay out the following sequence for the end of history.

This present time is an evil age, but soon will come a new, better age, filled with blessings and ruled by God (Introduction to Mark 13; see chapter 1, section 2). Before that age can come, there must be a dramatic time of judgment known as "the day of the Lord," and understood as the Second Coming of Christ (Introduction to James 5:7–9 [1.3]). In the last days before the Lord returns, evil will be rampant—the Temple will be destroyed (Mark 13:1–2 [8]); Rome will reign as a Beast (Introduction to Revelation 13 [44]); false teachers and prophets will mislead many (Revelation 16:13–16 [47]); and great persecution will befall the faithful (2 Timothy 3:1 [24]).

When the Lord returns, the dead will rise (Introduction to 1 Corinthians 15 [17]), Hell will cough up its residents (Revelation 9:1–2 [42]), and each will be judged (1 Corinthians 4:1–5 [16]). The mass of people will be divided, as wheat from tares (Matthew 13:24–30, 36–43 [4]). Christ will stand with the faithful (Romans 14:10–12 [15]), who have done their best in their lifetimes to live according to their calling (1 Peter 1:14–25), and who, by their prayers and preaching, have helped usher in this day (2 Peter 3:11–14 [31]). The wicked will go to destruction (Matthew 13:47–50 [5]), and the righteous to a wonderful, blissful existence (Introduction to Revelation 20 [48]).

No one knows the day or hour, save God alone (Matthew 24:3, 32–41 [7]), so each must live with the expectation that the day will come soon (Mark 13:28–37 [13]). In a real sense, the last days began with the earthly ministry of Jesus, and will continue until his return in glory. The Kingdom has started here, but will seek a final consummation in the next age. So with the author of Revelation, we boldly affirm, "Come, Lord Jesus" (Revelation 22:20 [52]).

At the Last Trumpet: Jesus Christ and the End of Time provides a harvest of the very best from this beloved Bible commentator. The meditations are arranged in biblical order and can be read for daily devotions, or straight through in one sitting. Some readers may be interested in reading through Barclay's writings topically, so a brief Topical Index of Passages concludes this volume.

As we near the end of one millennium, we do well to listen to Jesus' admonition, as recorded in Matthew 25:13. None of us, not even the favorite Scottish preacher William Barclay, knows the day or the hour. May these readings help the faithful to stay prepared and to keep awake.

Chris Conver

CHAPTER ONE

The Setting for the Presentation of the "End of Time" in the New Testament

The New Testament was written in a setting with existing ideas and notions about the end of time. In his discussions of several passages, Barclay lays out the configuration of this setting. Most prominent of these ideas are discussed under the following heads: The Jewish Ideas of the Messiah, The Things to Come, and Waiting for the Coming of the Lord.

1. The Jewish Ideas of the Messiah

[From Barclay's discussion of Mark 8:27–30]

Throughout all their existence the Jews never forgot that they were in a very special sense God's chosen people. Because of that, they naturally looked to a very special place in the world. In the early days they looked forward to achieving that position by what we might call natural means. They always regarded the greatest days in their history as the days of David; and they dreamed of a day when there would arise another king of David's line, a king who would make them great in righteousness and in power (Isaiah 9:7; 11:1; Jeremiah 22:4; 23:5; 30:9).

But as time went on it came to be pitilessly clear that this dreamed-of greatness would never be achieved by natural means. The ten tribes were carried off to Assyria and lost forever. The Babylonians conquered Jerusalem and carried the Jews away captive. Then came the Persians as their masters; then the Greeks; then the Romans. So far from knowing anything like dominion, for centuries the Jews never even knew what it was to be completely free and independent.

So another line of thought grew up. It is true that the idea of a great king of David's line never entirely vanished and was always intertwined in some way with their thought; but more and more they began to dream of a day when God would intervene in history and achieve by supernatural means that which natural means could never achieve. They looked for divine power to do what human power was helpless to do.

In between the Testaments were written a whole flood of books which were dreams and forecasts of this new age and the intervention of God. As a class they are called *apocalypses*. The word literally means *unveilings*. These books were meant to be unveilings of the future. It is to them that we must turn to find out what the Jews believed in the time of Jesus about the Messiah and the work of the Messiah and the new age. It is against their dreams that we must set the dream of Jesus.

In these books certain basic ideas occur. We follow here the classification of these ideas given by Schürer, who wrote *A History of the Jewish People in the Time of Jesus Christ*.

(i) Before the Messiah came there would be a time of terrible tribulation. There would be a Messianic travail. It would be the birth-pangs of a new age. Every conceivable terror would burst upon the world; every standard of honour and decency would be torn down; the world would become a physical and moral chaos.

> And honour shall be turned into shame,
> And strength humiliated into contempt,
> And probity destroyed,
> And beauty shall become ugliness . . .
> And envy shall rise in those who had not thought
> aught of themselves,
> And passion shall seize him that is peaceful,
> And many shall be stirred up in anger to injure many,
> And they shall rouse up armies in order to shed blood,
> And in the end they shall perish together with them.
>
> (*2 Baruch* 27)

There would be, "quakings of places, tumult of peoples, schemings of nations, confusion of leaders, disquietude of princes" (4 Ezra 9:3).

From heaven shall fall fiery words down to the earth. Lights shall come, bright and great, flashing into the midst of men; and earth, the universal mother, shall shake in these days at the hand of the Eternal. And the fishes of the sea and the beasts of the earth and the countless tribes of flying things and all the souls of men and every sea shall shudder at the presence of the Eternal and there shall be panic. And the towering mountain peaks and the hills of the giants he shall rend, and the murky abyss shall be visible to all. And the high ravines in the lofty mountains shall be full of dead bodies and rocks shall flow with blood and each torrent shall flood the plain. . . . And God shall judge all with war and sword, and there shall be brimstone from heaven, yea stones and rain and hail incessant and grievous. And death shall be upon the four-footed beasts. . . . Yea the land itself shall drink of the blood of the perishing and beasts shall eat their fill of flesh. (*Sibylline Oracles* 3:363ff.)

The Mishnah enumerates as signs that the coming of the Messiah is near,

That arrogance increases, ambition shoots up, that the vine yields fruit yet wine is dear. The government turns to heresy. There is no instruction. The synagogue is devoted to lewdness. Galilee is destroyed, Gablan laid waste. The inhabitants of a district go from city to city without finding compassion. The wisdom of the learned is hated, the godly despised, truth is absent. Boys insult old men, old men stand in the presence of children. The son depreciates the father, the daughter rebels against the mother, the daughter-in-law against the mother-in-law. A man's enemies are his house-fellows.

The time which preceded the coming of the Messiah was to be a time when the world was torn in pieces and every bond relaxed. The physical and the moral order would collapse.

(ii) Into this chaos there would come Elijah as the forerunner and herald of the Messiah. He was to heal the breaches and bring order into the chaos to prepare the way for the Messiah. In particular he was to mend disputes. In fact the Jewish oral law laid it down that money and property whose ownership was disputed, or anything found whose owner was unknown, must wait "till Elijah comes." When Elijah came the Messiah would not be far behind.

(iii) Then there would enter the Messiah. The word *Messiah* and the word *Christ* mean the same thing. *Messiah* is the Hebrew and *Christ* is the Greek for *the Anointed One.* A king was made king by anointing and the Messiah was God's Anointed King. It is important to remember that *Christ* is not a *name;* it is a *title.* Sometimes the Messiah was thought of as a king of David's line, but more often he was thought of as a great, superhuman figure crashing into history to remake the world and in the end to vindicate God's people.

(iv) The nations would ally themselves and gather themselves together against the champion of God.

> The kings of the nations shall throw themselves against this land bringing retribution on themselves. They shall seek to ravage the shrine of the mighty God and of the noblest men whensoever they come to the land. In a ring round the city the accursed kings shall place each one his throne with his infidel people by him. And then with a mighty voice God shall speak unto all the undisciplined, empty-minded people and judgment shall come upon them from the mighty God, and all shall perish at the hand of the Eternal. (*Sibylline Oracles* 3:663–672)

> It shall be that when all the nations hear his [the Messiah's] voice, every man shall leave his own land and the warfare they have one against the other, and an innumerable multitude

shall be gathered together desiring to fight against him. (4
Ezra 13:33–35)

(v) The result would be the total destruction of these hostile powers. Philo said that the Messiah would "take the field and make war
and destroy great and populous nations."

> He shall reprove them for their ungodliness,
> Rebuke them for their unrighteousness,
> Reproach them to their faces with their treacheries—
> And when he has rebuked them he shall destroy them.
>
> (4 Ezra 12:32, 33)

> And it shall come to pass in those days that none shall be saved,
> Either by gold or by silver,
> And none shall be able to escape.
> And there shall be no iron for war,
> Nor shall one clothe oneself with a breastplate.
> Bronze shall be of no service,
> And tin shall not be esteemed,
> And lead shall not be desired.
> And all things shall be destroyed from the surface of the earth.
>
> (*Enoch* 52:7–9)

The Messiah will be the most destructive conqueror in history,
smashing his enemies into utter extinction.

(vi) There would follow the renovation of Jerusalem. Sometimes
this was thought of as the purification of the existing city. More often
it was thought of as the coming down of the new Jerusalem from
heaven. The old house was to be folded up and carried away, and in
the new one, "All the pillars were new and the ornaments larger than
those of the first" (*Enoch* 90:28, 29).

(vii) The Jews who were dispersed all over the world would be
gathered into the city of the new Jerusalem. To this day the Jewish
daily prayer includes the petition, "Lift up a banner to gather our dispersed and assemble us from the four ends of the earth." The eleventh
of the *Psalms of Solomon* has a noble picture of that return.

Blow ye in Zion on the trumpet to summon the saints,
Cause ye to be heard in Jerusalem the voice of him that
bringeth good tidings;
For God hath had pity on Israel in visiting them.
Stand on the height, O Jerusalem, and behold thy children,
From the East and the West, gathered together by the Lord
From the North they come in the gladness of their God,
From the isles afar off God hath gathered them.
High mountains hath he abased into a plain for them;
The hills fled at their entrance.
The woods gave them shelter as they passed by;
Every sweet-smelling tree God caused to spring up for them,
That Israel might pass by in the visitation of the glory of their God.
Put on, O Jerusalem, thy glorious garments;
Make ready thy holy robe;
For God hath spoken good for Israel forever and ever,
Let the Lord do what he hath spoken concerning Israel and Jerusalem;
Let the Lord raise up Israel by his glorious name.
The mercy of the Lord be upon Israel forever and ever.

It can easily be seen how Jewish this new world was to be. The nationalistic element is dominant all the time.

(viii) Palestine would be the centre of the world and the rest of the world subject to it. All the nations would be subdued.

Sometimes it was thought of as a peaceful subjugation.

And all the isles and the cities shall say, How doth the Eternal love those men! For all things work in sympathy with them and help them. . . . Come let us all fall upon the earth and supplicate the eternal King, the mighty, everlasting God. Let us make procession to his Temple, for he is the sole Potentate. (*Sibylline Oracles* 3:690ff.)

More often the fate of the Gentiles was utter destruction at which Israel would exult and rejoice.

And he will appear to punish the Gentiles,

And he will destroy all their idols.

Then, thou, O Israel, shalt be happy.

And thou shalt mount upon the necks and the wings of the eagle

    [i.e., Rome, the eagle, is to be destroyed]

And they shall be ended and God will exalt thee.

. . . .

And thou shalt look from on high

And see thine enemies in Gehenna,

And thou shalt recognize them and rejoice.

(Assumption of Moses 10:8–10)

It was a grim picture. Israel would rejoice to see her enemies broken and in hell. Even the dead Israelites were to be raised up to share in the new world.

(ix) Finally, there would come the new age of peace and goodness which would last forever.

These are the Messianic ideas which were in the minds of men when Jesus came. They were violent, nationalistic, destructive, vengeful. True, they ended in the perfect reign of God, but they came to it through a bath of blood and a career of conquest. Think of Jesus set against a background like that. No wonder he had to re-educate his disciples in the meaning of Messiahship; and no wonder they crucified him in the end as a heretic. There was no room for a cross and there was little room for suffering love in a picture like that.

2. The Things to Come

[From Barclay's introduction to Mark 13]

Mark 13 is one of the most difficult chapters in the New Testament for a modern reader to understand. That is because it is one of the most Jewish chapters in the Bible. From beginning to end it is thinking in terms of Jewish history and Jewish ideas. All through it Jesus is using categories and pictures which were very familiar to the Jews of his day, but which are very strange, and indeed, unknown, to many modern readers. Even so, it is not possible to disregard this chapter because it is the source of many ideas about the Second Coming of Jesus. The difficulty about the doctrine of the Second Coming is that nowadays people are apt either completely to disregard it or to be so completely unbalanced about it that it becomes for them practically the only doctrine of the Christian faith. It may be that if we study this chapter with some care we shall come to a sane and correct view about this doctrine.

−The Day of the Lord

The Jews never doubted that they were the chosen people, and they never doubted that one day they would occupy the place in the world which the chosen people, as they saw it, deserved and were bound to have in the end. They had long since abandoned the idea that they could ever win that place by human means and they were confident that in the end God would directly intervene in history and win it for them. The day of God's intervention was *the day of the Lord.* Before that day of the Lord there would be a time of terror and trouble when the world would be shaken to its foundations and judgment would come. But it would be followed by the new world and the new age and the new glory.

In one sense this idea is the product of unconquerable *optimism.* The Jew was quite certain that God would break in. In another sense it was the product of bleak *pessimism,* because it was based on the idea that this world was so utterly bad that only its complete destruction and the emergence of a new world would suffice. They did not look for reformation. They looked for a re-creating of the entire scheme of things.

Let us look at some of the Old Testament passages about the day of the Lord. Amos writes (5:16–20):

> In all the squares there shall be wailing; and in all the streets they shall say, 'Alas! Alas!' They shall call the farmers to mourning and to wailing those who are skilled in lamentations, and in all vineyards there shall be wailing, for I will pass through the midst of you, says the Lord. Woe to you who

desire the day of the Lord! Why would you have the day of the Lord? It is darkness, and not light . . . gloom with no brightness in it.

Isaiah (13:6–16) has a terrible passage about the day of the Lord:

Wail! for the day of the Lord is near. As destruction from the Almighty it will come. . . . Behold the day of the Lord comes, cruel with wrath and fierce anger, to make the earth a desolation, and to destroy its sinners from it. For the stars of the heavens and their constellations will not give their light. The sun will be dark at its rising and the moon will not shed its light. . . . Therefore I will make the heavens tremble, and the earth will be shaken out of its place, at the wrath of the Lord of Hosts, in the day of his fierce anger. . . .

The second and third chapters of Joel are full of terrible descriptions of the day of the Lord:

The day of the Lord is coming . . . a day of darkness and gloom, a day of clouds and thick darkness. . . . I will give portents in the heavens and on the earth, blood and fire, and columns of smoke. The sun shall be turned to darkness and the moon to blood, before the great and terrible day of the Lord comes.

Again and again such passages of terror meet us in the Old Testament. The day of the Lord will be sudden, shattering, terrifying. The word will reel with destruction. The very course of nature will be uprooted, and God, the judge, will come.

Between the Old and the New Testaments there was a time when the Jews knew no freedom. It was therefore only natural that their hopes and dreams of the day of the Lord would become even more vivid. In that time a kind of popular religious literature grew up. Jesus would know it. All the Jews would be familiar with its picture. The writings of which this literature consisted were called *apocalypses.* These books were dreams and visions of what would happen when the day of the Lord came and in the terrible time immediately before it. They continued to use the Old Testament imagery, and to supplement it with new details. But, it must be noted, all these books were dreams and visions. They were attempts to paint the unpaintable and to speak the unspeakable. They were poetry, not prose. They were visions, not science. They were dreams, not history. They were never meant to be taken prosaically as maps of the future and timetables of events to come.

We will see that every single detail can be paralleled in the visions of the Old Testament and of the literature between the Testaments. Jesus was taking the language, the imagery, the apparatus of apocalyptic literature, and using it to try to make people understand. He was working with the only ideas that people knew. But he knew, as they knew, that these things were only pictures, for no man could really tell what would happen when God broke in.

—The Different Strands

Further, there are various strands of thought. The Gospel writers had a way of collecting Jesus' sayings on any subject. It was a wise way to write and excellent for teaching purposes. Here Mark, as it were, collects *Jesus' sayings about the future.* Now even a cursory reading, with no special knowledge, shows that, though all these sayings were about the future, they were not all about the same things. There are in fact *five* different strands.

(i) *There are prophecies of the destruction of Jerusalem.* Jesus foresaw the end of the holy city. As we shall see, Jesus was right. Jerusalem fell in A.D. 70. The Temple was destroyed and the most terrible things happened.

(ii) *There is warning of persecution to come.* Jesus foresaw that his followers would have to go through the most heart-breaking and soul-searing experiences, and he warned them in advance.

(iii) *There are warnings of the dangers of the last days.* Jesus saw quite clearly that men would come who would twist and adulterate the Christian faith. It was bound to be so, for men are always inclined to listen to their own proud minds rather than to the voice of God. He wished to defend his people in advance from the heresies and lies which would invade the church.

(iv) *There are warnings of the Second Coming.* Now, these warnings of the Second Coming are dressed in the language which has to do with the day of the Lord. The imagery of the day of the Lord and of the Second Coming are inextricably mixed up. It had to be so, because no man could possibly know what would happen in either case. It is with visions and dreams that we have to deal. The only pictures Jesus could use about his Second Coming were those which prophets and apocalyptists had already used about the day of the Lord. They are not meant to be taken literally. They are meant as impressionistic pictures, as seer's visions, designed to impress upon men the greatness of that event when it should come.

(v) *There are warnings of the necessity to be on the watch.* If men live in the shadow of eternity, if they live with the constant possibility of the intervention of God, if they live with the prospect of the consummation of the coming of Christ ever before them, if the times and the seasons are known only to God, there is the necessity ever to be ready.

3. Waiting for the Coming of the Lord

[From Barclay's discussion of James 5:7–9]

It so happened that the early church was mistaken. Jesus Christ did not return within a generation. But it will be of interest to gather up the New Testament's teaching about the Second Coming so that we may see the essential truth at its heart.

We may first note that the New Testament uses three different words to describe the Second Coming of Jesus Christ.

(i) The commonest is *parousia,* a word which has come into English as it stands. It is used in Matthew 24:3, 27, 37, 39; 1 Thessalonians 2:19; 3:13; 4:15; 5:23; 2 Thessalonians 2:1; 1 Corinthians 15:23; 1 John 2:28; 2 Peter 1:16; 3:4. In secular Greek this is the ordinary word for someone's presence or arrival. But it has two other usages, one of which became quite technical. It is used of the invasion of a country by an army; and specially it is used of the visit of a king or a governor to a province of his empire. So, then, when this word is used of Jesus, it means that his Second Coming is the final invasion of earth by heaven and the coming of the King to receive the final submission and adoration of his subjects.

(ii) The New Testament also uses the word *epiphaneia* (Titus 2:13; 2 Timothy 4:1; 2 Thessalonians 2:9). In ordinary Greek this word has two special usages. It is used of the appearance of a god to his worshipper; and it is used of the accession of an emperor to the imperial power of Rome. So, then, when this word is used of Jesus, it means that his Second Coming is God appearing to his people, both to those who are waiting for him and to those who are disregarding him.

(iii) Finally the New Testament uses the word *apokalupsis* (1 Peter 1:7, 13). *Apokalupsis* in ordinary Greek means an *unveiling* or a *laying bare;* and when it is used of Jesus, it means that his Second Coming is the laying bare of the power and glory of God come upon men.

Here, then, we have a series of great pictures. The Second Coming of Jesus is the arrival of the King; it is God appearing to his people and mounting his eternal throne; it is God directing on the world the full blaze of his heavenly glory.

We may now gather up briefly the teaching of the New Testament about the Second Coming and the various uses it makes of the idea.

(i) The New Testament is clear that no man knows the day or the hour when Christ comes again. So secret, in fact, is that time that Jesus himself does not know it; it is known to God alone (Matthew 24:36; Mark 13:32). From this basic fact one thing is clear. Human speculation about the time of the Second Coming is not only useless, it is blasphemous; for surely no man should seek to gain a knowledge which is hidden from Jesus Christ himself and resides only in the mind of God.

(ii) The one thing that the New Testament does say about the Second Coming is that it will be as sudden as the lightning and as unexpected as a thief in the night (Matthew 24:27, 37, 39; 1 Thessalonians

5:2; 2 Peter 3:10). We cannot wait to get ready when it comes; we must be ready for its coming.

So, the New Testament urges certain duties upon men.

(i) They must be for ever on the watch (1 Peter 4:7). They are like servants whose master has gone away and who, not knowing when he will return, must have everything ready for his return, whether it be at morning, at midday, or at evening (Matthew 24:36–51).

(ii) Long delay must not produce despair or forgetfulness (2 Peter 3:4). God does not see time as men do. To him a thousand years are as a watch in the night and even if the years pass on, it does not mean that he has either changed or abandoned his design.

(iii) Men must use the time given them to prepare for the coming of the King. They must be sober (1 Peter 4:7). They must get to themselves holiness (1 Thessalonians 3:13). By the grace of God they must become blameless in body and in spirit (1 Thessalonians 5:23). They must put off the works of darkness and put on the armour of light now that the day is far spent (Romans 13:11–14). Men must use the time given them to make themselves such that they can greet the coming of the King with joy and without shame.

(iv) When that time comes, they must be found in fellowship. Peter uses the thought of the Second Coming to urge men to love and mutual hospitality (1 Peter 4:8, 9). Paul commands that all things be done in love—*Maran atha*—the Lord is at hand (1 Corinthians 16:14, 22). He says that our *forbearance* must be known to all men because the Lord is at hand (Philippians 4:5). The word translated *forbearance* is *epieikes* which means the spirit that is more ready to offer forgiveness than to demand justice. The writer to the Hebrews demands mutual help, mutual Christian fellowship, mutual encouragement because the day is coming near (Hebrews 10:24, 25). The New Testament is sure that in view of the coming of Christ we must have our personal relationships right with our fellowmen. The New Testament would urge that no man ought to end a day with an unhealed breach between himself and a fellowman, lest in the night Christ should come.

(v) John uses the Second Coming as a reason for urging men to abide in Christ (1 John 2:28). Surely the best preparation for meeting Christ is to live close to him every day.

Much of the imagery attached to the Second Coming is Jewish, part of the traditional apparatus of the last things in the ancient Jewish mind. There are many things which we are not meant to take literally. But the great truth behind all the temporary pictures of the Second Coming is that this world is not purposeless but going somewhere, that there is one divine far-off event to which the whole creation moves.

CHAPTER TWO

The Messianic Banquet
Matthew 8:5–13

Here Jesus uses a famous and vivid Jewish picture. The Jews believed that when the Messiah came there would be a great banquet at which all Jews would sit down to feast. Behemoth, the greatest of the land beasts, and leviathan, the greatest of the denizens of the sea, would provide the fare for the banqueters. "Thou has reserved them to be devoured by whom Thou wilt and when" (4 Ezra 6:52). "And behemoth shall be revealed from his place, and leviathan shall ascend from the sea, those two great monsters which I created on the fifth day of creation, and shall have kept until that time; and then shall they be food for all that are left" (2 Baruch 29:4).

The Jews looked forward with all their hearts to this Messianic banquet; but it never for a moment crossed their minds that any Gentile would ever sit down at it. By that time the Gentiles would have been destroyed. "The nation and kingdom that will not serve you shall perish; those nations shall be utterly laid waste" (Isaiah 60:12). Yet here is Jesus saying that many shall come from the east and from the west, and sit down at table at that banquet.

Still worse, he says that many of the sons of the kingdom will be shut out. A son is an heir; therefore the son of the kingdom is the man who is to inherit the kingdom, for the son is always heir; but the Jews are to lose their inheritance. Always in Jewish thought "the inheritance of sinners is darkness" (Psalms of Solomon 15:11). The rabbis had a saying, "The sinners in Gehenna will be covered with darkness." To the Jew the extraordinary and the shattering thing about all this was that the Gentile, whom he expected to be absolutely shut out, was to be a guest at the Messianic banquet, and the Jew, whom he expected to be welcomed with open arms, is to be shut out in the outer darkness. The tables were to be turned, and all expectations were to be reversed.

The Jew had to learn that the passport to God's presence is not membership of any nation; it is faith. The Jew believed that he belonged to the chosen people and that because he was a Jew he was therefore dear to God. He belonged to God's *herrenvolk,* and that was enough automatically to gain him salvation. Jesus taught that the only aristocracy in the Kingdom of God is the aristocracy of faith. Jesus Christ is not the possession of any one race of men; Jesus Christ is the possession of every man in every race in whose heart there is faith.

CHAPTER THREE

The Challenge of the King
to His Messengers

Matthew 10:16–23

We must note that in these words Jesus was making use of ideas and pictures which were part and parcel of Jewish thought. We have seen again and again how it was the custom of the Jews, in their pictures of the future, to divide time into two ages. There was the present age, which is wholly bad; there was the age to come, which would be the golden age of God; and in between there was the day of the Lord, which would be a terrible time of chaos and destruction and judgment. Now in Jewish thought one of the ever-recurring features of the day of the Lord was that it would split friends and kindred into two, and that the dearest bonds of earth would be destroyed in bitter enmities.

When Jesus spoke of the terrors to come, and of the divisions which would tear apart the closest of ties of earth, he was in effect saying: "The day of the Lord has come." And his men would know that he was saying this, and would go out in the knowledge that they were living in the greatest days of history.

This passage contains one strange saying which we cannot honestly neglect. Matthew depicts Jesus as sending out his men, and, as he does so, saying to them, "You will not complete your tour of the cities of Israel, until the Son of Man shall come." On the face of it that seems to mean that before his men had completed their preaching tour, his day of glory and his return to power would have taken place. The difficulty is just this—that did not in fact happen, and, if at that moment, Jesus had that expectation, he was mistaken. If he said this in this way, he foretold something which actually did not happen. But there is a perfectly good and sufficient explanation of this apparent difficulty.

The people of the early church believed intensely in the Second Coming of Jesus, and they believed it would happen soon, certainly within their own lifetime. There could be nothing more natural than that, because they were living in days of savage persecution, and they were longing for the day of their release and their glory. The result was that they fastened on every possible saying of Jesus which could be interpreted as foretelling his triumphant and glorious return; and sometimes they quite naturally used things which Jesus said, and read into them something more definite than was originally there.

We can see this process happening within the pages of the New Testament itself. There are three versions of the one saying of Jesus. Let us set them down one after another:

> Truly, I say to you, there are some standing here who will not taste death before they see the Son of Man coming in his Kingdom. (Matthew 16:28)

> Truly, I say to you, there are some standing here who will not taste death before they see the Kingdom of God come with power. (Mark 9:1)

> But I tell you truly, there are some standing here who will not taste death before they see the kingdom of God. (Luke 9:27)

Now it is clear that these are three versions of the same saying. Mark is the earliest Gospel, and therefore Mark's version is most likely to be strictly accurate. Mark says that there were some listening to Jesus who would not die until they saw the Kingdom of God coming with power. That was gloriously true, for within thirty years of the cross the message of Crucified and Risen Christ had swept across the world and had reached Rome, the capital of the world. Indeed men were being swept into the Kingdom; indeed the Kingdom was coming with power. Luke transmits the saying in the same way as Mark.

Now look at Matthew. His version is slightly different; he says that there are some who will not die until they see the Son of Man coming in power. That, in fact, did not happen. The explanation is that Matthew was writing between A.D. 80 and 90, in days when terrible persecution was raging. Men were clutching at everything which promised release from agony; and he took a saying which foretold the spread of the Kingdom and turned it into a saying which foretold the return of Christ within a lifetime—and who shall blame him?

This is what Matthew has done here. Take this saying in our passage and write it as Mark or Luke would have written it: "You will not complete your tour of the cities of Israel, until the *Kingdom of God* shall come." That was blessedly true, for as the tour went on, men's hearts opened to Jesus Christ, and they took him as Master and Lord.

In a passage like this we must not think of Jesus as mistaken; we must rather think that Matthew read into a promise of the coming of the Kingdom a promise of the Second Coming of Jesus Christ. And he did so because, in days of terror, men clutched at the hope of Christ; and Christ did come to them in the Spirit, for no man ever suffered alone for Christ.

CHAPTER FOUR

The Act of an Enemy

Matthew 13:24–30, 36–43

In its lessons this is one of the most practical parables Jesus ever told.

(i) It teaches us that there is always a hostile power in the world, seeking and waiting to destroy the good seed. Our experience is that both kinds of influence act upon our lives, the influence which helps the seed of the word to flourish and to grow, and the influence which seeks to destroy the good seed before it can produce fruit at all. The lesson is that we must be for ever on our guard.

(ii) It teaches us how hard it is to distinguish between those who are in the Kingdom and those who are not. A man may appear to be good and may in fact be bad; and a man may appear to be bad and may yet be good. We are much too quick to classify people and label them good or bad without knowing all the facts.

(iii) It teaches us not to be so quick with our judgments. If the reapers had had their way, they would have tried to tear out the darnel and they would have torn out the wheat as well. Judgment had to wait until the harvest came. A man in the end will be judged, not by any single act or stage in his life, but by his whole life. Judgment cannot come until the end. A man may make a great mistake, and then redeem himself and, by the grace of God, atone for it by making the rest of life a lovely thing. A man may live an honourable life and then in the end wreck it all by a sudden collapse into sin. No one who sees only part of a thing can judge the whole; and no one who knows only part of a man's life can judge the whole man.

(iv) It teaches us that judgment does come in the end. Judgment is not hasty, but judgment comes. It may be that, humanly speaking, in this life the sinner seems to escape the consequences, but there is a life to come. It may be that, humanly speaking, goodness never seems to enter into its reward, but there is a new world to redress the balance of the old.

(v) It teaches us that the only person with the right to judge is God. It is God alone who can discern the good and the bad; it is God alone who sees all of a man and all of his life. It is God alone who can judge.

So, then, ultimately this parable is two things—it is a warning not to judge people at all, and it is a warning that in the end there comes the judgment of God.

CHAPTER FIVE

The Catch and the Separation

Matthew 13:47–50

There are two great lessons in this parable.

(i) It is in the nature of the drag-net that it does not, and cannot, discriminate. It is bound to draw in all kinds of things in its course through the water. Its contents are bound to be a mixture. If we apply that to the church, which is the instrument of God's Kingdom upon earth, it means that the church cannot be discriminative but is bound to be a mixture of all kinds of people, good and bad, useless and useful.

There have always been two views of the church—the exclusive and the inclusive. The exclusive view holds that the church is for people who are good, people who are really and fully committed, people who are quite different from the world. There is an attraction in that view, but it is not the New Testament view, because, apart from anything else, *who is to do the judging,* when we are told that we must not judge? (Matthew 7:1.) It is not any man's place to say who is committed to Christ and who is not. The inclusive view feels instinctively that the church must be open to all, and that, like the drag-net, so long as it is a human institution it is bound to be a mixture. That is exactly what this parable teaches.

(ii) But equally this parable teaches that the time of separation will come when the good and the bad are sent to their respective destinations. That separation, however, certain as it is, is not man's work but God's. Therefore it is our duty to gather in all who will come, and not to judge or separate, but to leave the final judgment to God.

CHAPTER SIX

The Warning and the Promise

Matthew 16:27–28

There are two quite distinct sayings here.

(i) The first is a *warning,* the warning of inevitable judgment. Life is going somewhere—and life is going to judgment. In any sphere of life there inevitably comes the day of reckoning. There is no escape from the fact that Christianity teaches that after life there comes the judgment; and when we take this passage in conjunction with the passage which goes before, we see at once what the standard of judgment is. The man who selfishly hugs life to himself, the man whose first concern is his own safety, his own security and his own comfort, is in heaven's eyes the failure, however rich and successful and prosperous he may seem to be. The man who spends himself for others, and who lives life as a gallant adventure, is the man who receives heaven's praise and God's reward.

(ii) The second is a *promise.* As Matthew records this phrase, it reads as if Jesus spoke as if he expected his own visible return in the lifetime of some of those who were listening to him. If Jesus said that he was mistaken. But we see the real meaning of what Jesus said when we turn to Mark's record of it. Mark has: And he said to them, "Truly, I say to you, there are some standing here who will not taste death before they see the Kingdom of God come with power" (Mark 9:1).

It is of the mighty working of his kingdom that Jesus is speaking; and what he said came most divinely true. There were those standing there who saw the coming of Jesus in the coming of the Spirit at the day of Pentecost. There were those who were to see Gentile and Jew swept into the Kingdom; they were to see the tide of the Christian message sweep across Asia Minor and cover Europe until it reached Rome. Well within the lifetime of those who heard Jesus speak, the Kingdom came with power.

CHAPTER SEVEN

The Coming of the King

Matthew 24:3, 32–41

Here Jesus speaks of his Second Coming directly. The New Testament does not ever use the phrase *the Second Coming*. The word which it uses to describe the return of Christ in glory is interesting. It is *parousia;* this word has come into English as a description of the Second Coming; it is quite common in the rest of the New Testament, but in the Gospels this is the only chapter in which it occurs (verses 3, 27, 37, 39). The interesting thing is that it is the regular word for the arrival of a governor into his province or for the coming of a king to his subjects. It regularly describes a coming in authority and in power.

The remainder of this chapter will have much to tell us about it, but at the moment we note that, whatever else is true about the doctrine of the Second Coming, it certainly conserves two great facts.

(i) It conserves the fact of the ultimate triumph of Christ. He whom men crucified on a cross will one day be the Lord of all men. For Jesus Christ the end is sure—and that end is his universal kingship.

(ii) It conserves the fact that history is going somewhere. Sometimes men have felt that history was plunging to an ever wilder and wilder chaos, that it is nothing more than "the record of the sins and follies of men." Sometimes men have felt that history was cyclic and that the same weary round of things would happen over and over again. The Stoics believed that there are certain fixed periods, that at the end of each the world is destroyed in a great conflagration; and that then the same story in every littlest detail takes place all over again. This is a grim thought that men are bound to an eternal tread-mill in which there is no progress and from which there is no escape.

But the Second Coming has in it this essential truth—that there is "one divine far-off event, to which the whole creation moves," and that event is not dissolution but the universal and eternal rule of God.

Verses 36–41 refer to the Second Coming; and they tell us certain most important truths.

(i) They tell us that the hour of that event is known to God and to God alone. It is, therefore, clear that speculation regarding the time of the Second Coming is nothing less than blasphemy, for the man who so speculates is seeking to wrest from God secrets which belong to God alone. It is not any man's duty to speculate; it is his duty to prepare himself, and to watch.

(ii) They tell us that that time will come with shattering sudden-ness on those who are immersed in material things. In the old story Noah prepared himself in the calm weather for the flood which was to come, and when it came he was ready. But the rest of mankind were lost in their eating and drinking and marrying and giving in marriage, and were caught completely unawares, and were therefore swept away. These verses are a warning never to become so immersed in time that we forget eternity, never to let our concern with worldly affairs, how-ever necessary, completely distract us from remembering that there is a God, that the issues of life and death are in his hands, and that whenever his call comes, at morning, at midday, or at evening, it must find us ready.

(iii) They tell us that the coming of Christ will be a time of sepa-ration and of judgment, when he will gather to himself those who are his own.

CHAPTER EIGHT

The Goal in Life Worth Any Sacrifice

Mark 9:43–48

The Jewish rabbis had sayings based on the way in which some parts of the body can lend themselves to sin. "The eye and the heart are the two brokers of sin." "The eye and the heart are the two handmaids of sin." "Passions lodge only in him who sees." "Woe to him who goes after his eyes for the eyes are adulterous." There are certain instincts in man, and certain parts of man's physical constitution, which minister to sin. This saying of Jesus is not to be taken literally, but is a vivid eastern way of saying that there is a goal in life worth any sacrifice to attain it.

There are in this passage repeated references to *Gehenna. Gehenna* is spoken of in the New Testament in Matthew 5:22, 29, 30; 10:28; 18:9; 23:15, 33; Luke 12:5; James 3:6. The word is regularly translated *Hell.* It is a word with a history. It is a form of the word *Hinnom.* The valley of Hinnom was a ravine outside Jerusalem. It had an evil past.

It was the valley in which Ahaz, in the old days, had instituted fire worship and the sacrifice of little children in the fire. "He burned incense in the valley of the son of Hinnom, and burned his sons as an offering" (2 Chronicles 28:3). That terrible heathen worship was also followed by Manasseh (2 Chronicles 33:6). The valley of Hinnom, Gehenna, therefore, was the scene of one of Israel's most terrible lapses into heathen customs. In his reformations Josiah declared it an unclean place. "He defiled Topheth, which is in the valley of the sons of Hinnom, that no one might burn his son or his daughter as an offering to Molech" (2 Kings 23:10).

When the valley had been so declared unclean and had been so desecrated it was set apart as the place where the refuse of Jerusalem was burned. The consequence was that it was a foul, unclean place, where loathsome worms bred on the refuse, and which smoked and smouldered at all times like some vast incinerator. The actual phrase about the worm which does not die, and the fire which is not quenched, comes from a description of the fate of Israel's evil enemies in Isaiah 66:24.

Because of all this Gehenna had become a kind of type or symbol of Hell, the place where the souls of the wicked would be tortured and destroyed. It is so used in the Talmud. "The sinner who desists from the words of the Law will in the end inherit Gehenna." So then Gehenna stands as the place of punishment, and the word roused in the mind of every Israelite the grimmest and most terrible pictures.

CHAPTER NINE

A City's Doom

Mark 13:1–2

We begin with the prophecies of Jesus which foretold the doom of Jerusalem. The Temple which Herod built was one of the wonders of the world. It was begun in 20–19 B.C. and in the time of Jesus was not yet completely finished. It was built on the top of Mount Moriah. Instead of levelling off the summit of the mountain a kind of vast platform was formed by raising up walls of massive masonry and enclosing the whole area. On these walls a platform was laid, strengthened by piers which distributed the weight of the superstructure. Josephus tells us that some of these stones were forty feet long by twelve feet high by eighteen feet wide. It would be some of these vast stones that moved the Galilaean disciples to such wondering amazement.

The most magnificent entrance to the Temple was at the southwest angle. Here between the city and the Temple hill there stretched the Tyropoeon Valley. A marvellous bridge spanned the valley. Each arch was forty-one and a half feet and there were stones used in the building of it which measured twenty-four feet long. The Tyropoeon Valley was no less than two hundred and twenty-five feet below. The breadth of the cleft that the bridge spanned was three hundred and fifty-four feet, and the bridge itself was fifty feet in breadth. The bridge led straight into the Royal Porch. The porch consisted of a double row of Corinthian pillars all thirty-seven and a half feet high and each one cut out of one solid block of marble.

It was all this splendour that so impressed the disciples. The Temple seemed the summit of human art and achievement, and seemed so vast and solid that it would stand for ever. But Jesus made the astonishing statement that the day was coming when not one of these stones would stand upon another. In less then fifty years his prophecy came tragically true.

CHAPTER TEN

His Coming Again

Mark 13:7–8, 24–27

Here Jesus unmistakably speaks of his coming again. But—and this is important—he clothes the idea in three pictures which are part and parcel of the apparatus connected with the day of the Lord.

(i) The day of the Lord was to be preceded by a time of wars. Fourth Ezra declares that before the day of the Lord there will be,

> Quakings of places
> Tumult of peoples,
> Scheming of nations,
> Confusion of leaders,
> Disquietude of princes.
>   (9:3)

The same book says,

> And there shall come astonishment of mind upon the dwellers on earth. And they shall plan to war one against another, city against city, place against place, people against people, and kingdom against kingdom. (13:31)

The Sibylline Oracles foresee that,

> King captures king and takes his land, and nations ravage nations and potentates people, and rulers all flee to another land,

and the land is changed in men and a barbarian empire ravages Hellas and drains the rich land of its wealth, and men come face to face in strife. (3:633–647)

Second Baruch has the same ideas. In 27:2–13 this book singles out twelve things which will precede the new age.

In the first part there will be the beginning of commotions. In the second part there shall be the slayings of great ones. In the third part the fall of many by death. In the fourth part the sending of the sword. In the fifth part famine and withholding of rain. In the sixth part earthquakes and terrors. . . . In the eighth part a multitude of spectres and attacks of the evil spirits. In the ninth part the fall of fire. In the tenth part rapine and much oppression. In the eleventh part wickedness and unchastity. In the twelfth part confusion from the mingling together of all those things aforesaid.

All the inhabitants of the earth shall be moved against one another. (*2 Baruch* 48:32)

And they shall hate one another,
And provoke one another to fight.

. . . .

And it shall come to pass that whosoever comes safe out of the war shall die in the earthquake,
And whosoever gets safe out of the earthquake shall be burned by the fire,
And whosoever gets safe out of the fire shall be destroyed by famine.

It is abundantly clear that when Jesus spoke of wars and rumours of wars he was using pictures which were part and parcel of Jewish dreams of the future.

(ii) The day of the Lord was to be preceded by the darkening of sun and moon. The Old Testament itself is full of that (Amos 8:9; Joel 2:10; 3:15; Ezekiel 32:7, 8; Isaiah 13:10; 34:4); again the popular literature of Jesus' day is full of it, too.

Then shall the sun suddenly shine forth by night,
And the moon by day.
. . . .
The outgoings of the stars shall change.

(4 Ezra 5:4–7)

Second Baruch 32:1 speaks of "the time in which the mighty one is to shake the whole creation." The *Sibylline Oracles* (3:796–806) talk of a time when "swords in the star-lit heaven appear by night towards dusk and towards dawn . . . and all the brightness of the sun fails at midday from the heaven, and the moon's rays shine forth and come back to earth, and a sign comes from the rocks with dripping streams of blood." The *Assumption of Moses* foresees a time when:

The horns of the sun shall be broken and he shall be turned into darkness,
And the moon shall not give her light, and be turned wholly into blood,
And the circle of the stars shall be disturbed.

(10:5)

Once again it is clear that Jesus is using the popular language which everyone knew.

(iii) It was a regular part of the imagery that the Jews were to be gathered back to Palestine from the four corners of the earth. The Old Testament itself is full of that idea (Isaiah 27:13; 35:8–10; Micah 7:12; Zechariah 10:6–11); once more the popular literature loves the idea:

Blow ye in Zion on the trumpet to summon the saints,
Cause ye to be heard in Jerusalem the voice of him that bringeth good tidings,
For God hath had pity on Israel in visiting them.
Stand on the height, O Jerusalem, and behold thy children.
From the East and the West gathered together by the Lord.

(*Psalms of Solomon* 11:1–3)

The Lord will gather you together in faith through His tender mercy, and for the sake of Abraham and Isaac and Jacob. (*Testament of Asher* 7:5–7)

When we read the pictorial words of Jesus about the Second Coming we must remember that he is giving us neither a map of eternity nor a timetable to the future, but that he is simply using the language and the pictures that many a Jew knew and used for centuries before him.

But it is extremely interesting to note that the things Jesus prophesied were in fact happening. He prophesied wars and the dreaded Parthians were in fact pressing in on the Roman frontiers. He prophesied earthquakes and within forty years the Roman world was aghast at the earthquake which devastated Laodicaea and by the eruption of Vesuvius which buried Pompeii in lava. He prophesied famines, and there was famine in Rome in the days of Claudius. It was in fact such a time of terror in the near future that when Tacitus began his histories he said that everything happening seemed to prove that the gods were seeking, not salvation, but vengeance on the Roman Empire.

In this passage the one thing that we must retain is the fact that Jesus did foretell that he would come again.

CHAPTER ELEVEN

The Hard Way

Mark 13:9–13

Now we come to the warnings of persecution to come. Jesus never left his followers in any doubt that they had chosen a hard way. No man could say that he had not known the conditions of Christ's service in advance.

The handing over to councils and the scourging in synagogues refer to Jewish persecution. In Jerusalem there was the great Sanhedrin, the supreme court of the Jews, but every town and village had its local Sanhedrin. Before such local Sanhedrins the self-confessed heretics would be tried, and in the synagogues they would be publicly scourged. The governors and kings refer to trials before the Roman courts, such as Paul faced before Felix and Festus and Agrippa.

It was a fact that the Christians were wonderfully strengthened in their trials. When we read of the trials of the martyrs, even though they were often ignorant and unlettered men, the impression often is that it was the judges and not the Christians who were on trial. Their Christian faith enabled the simplest folk to fear God so much that they never feared the face of any man.

It was true that even those of a man's own family sometimes betrayed him. In the early Roman Empire one of the curses was the informer (*delator*). There were those who, in their attempts to curry favour with the authorities, would not hesitate to betray their own kith and kin. That must have been the sorest blow of all.

In Hitler's Germany a man was arrested because he stood for freedom. He endured imprisonment and torture with stoic and uncomplaining fortitude. Finally, with spirit still unbroken, he was released. Some short time afterwards he committed suicide. Many wondered why. Those who knew him well knew the reason—he had discovered that his own son was the person who had informed against him. The treachery of his own broke him in a way that the cruelty of his enemies was unable to achieve.

This family and domestic hostility was one of the regular items in the catalogue of terror of the last and terrible days. "Friends shall attack one another suddenly" (4 Esdras 5:9). "And they shall hate one another and provoke one another to fight" (*2 Baruch* 70:3). "And they shall strive with one another, the young with the old, and the old with the young, the poor with the rich, the lowly with the great, the beggar with the prince" (*Jubilees* 23:19). "Children shall shame the elders, and the elders shall rise up before the children" (The Mishnah, *Sotah* 9:15). "For the son treats the father with contempt, the daughter rises up against her mother, the daughter-in-law against her mother-in-law. A man's enemies are the men of his own house" (Micah 7:6).

Life becomes a hell upon earth when personal loyalties are destroyed and when there is no love which a man may trust.

It was true that the Christians were hated. Tacitus talked of Christianity as an accursed superstition; Suetonius called it a new and evil superstition. The main reason for the hatred was the way in which Christianity cut across family ties. The fact was that a man had to love Christ more than father or mother, or son or daughter. And the matter was complicated by the way that the Christians were much slandered. It is beyond doubt that the Jews did much to encourage these slanders.

In this, as in all other things, it is the man who endures to the end who is saved. Life is not a short, sharp sprint; it is a marathon race. Life is not a single battle; it is a long campaign. Dr. G. J. Jeffrey tells of a famous man who refused to have his biography written when he was still alive. "I have seen too many men fall out on the last lap of the race," he said. Life is never safe until it reaches journey's end. It was Bunyan who, in his dream, saw that from the very gates of heaven there was a way to hell. It is the man who endures *to the end* who will be saved.

CHAPTER TWELVE

A City's Agony

Mark 13:14–20

Jesus forecasts some of the awful terror of the siege and the final fall of Jerusalem. It is his warning that when the first signs of it came people ought to flee, not even waiting to pick up their clothes or to try to save their goods. In fact the people did precisely the opposite. They crowded into Jerusalem, and death came in ways that are almost too terrible to think about.

The phrase *the abomination of desolation* has its origin in the book of Daniel (Daniel 9:27; 11:31; 12:11). The Hebrew expression literally means *the profanation that appals.* The origin of the phrase was in connection with Antiocheius. We have already seen that he tried to stamp out the Jewish religion and introduce Greek thought and Greek ways.

He desecrated the Temple by offering swine's flesh on the great altar and by setting up public brothels in the sacred courts. Before the very Holy Place itself he set up a great statue of Olympian Zeus and ordered the Jews to worship it. In connection with that the writer of First Maccabees says (1:54), "Now the fifteenth day of the month Casleu, in the hundred and forty-fifth year, they set up the abomination of desolation upon the altar and builded idol altars throughout the cities of Judah on every side." The phrase *the abomination of desolation, the profanation that appals,* originally described the heathen image and all that accompanied it with which Antiocheius desecrated the Temple. Jesus prophesies that the same kind of thing is going to happen again. It very nearly happened in the year A.D. 40. Caligula was then Roman Emperor. He was an epileptic and mad. But he insisted that he was a god. He heard of the imageless worship of the Temple of Jerusalem and planned to set up his own statue in the Holy Place. His advisers besought him not to do so, for they knew that, if he did, a bloody civil war would result. He was obstinate, but fortunately he died in A.D. 41 before he could carry out his plan of desecration.

What does Jesus mean when he speaks about *the abomination of desolation?* Men expected not only a Messiah, but also the emergence of a power who would be the very incarnation of evil and who would gather up into himself everything that was against God. Paul called that power *the Man of Lawlessness* (2 Thessalonians 2:3). John of the Revelation identified that power with Rome (Revelation 17). Jesus is saying, "Some day, quite soon, you will see the very incarnate power of evil rise up in a deliberate attempt to destroy the people and the Holy Place of God." He takes the old phrase and uses it to describe the terrible things that are about to happen.

It was in A.D. 70 that Jerusalem finally fell to the besieging army of Titus, who was to be Emperor of Rome. The horrors of that siege form one of the grimmest pages in history. The people crowded into Jerusalem from the countryside. Titus had no alternative but to starve the city into subjection. The matter was complicated by the fact that even at that terrible time there were sects and factions inside the city itself. Jerusalem was torn without and within.

The prophecy that Jesus made of terrible days ahead for Jerusalem came most abundantly true. Those who crowded into the city for safety died by the hundred thousand, and only those who took his advice and fled to the hills were saved.

CHAPTER THIRTEEN

Be on the Watch

Mark 13:28–37

There are three special things to note in this passage.

(i) It is sometimes held that when Jesus said that these things were to happen within this generation he was in error. But Jesus was right, for this sentence does not refer to the Second Coming. It could not when the next sentence says he does not know when that day will be. It refers to Jesus' prophecies about the fall of Jerusalem and the destruction of the Temple and they were abundantly fulfilled.

(ii) Jesus says that he does not know the day or the hour when he will come again. There were things which even he left without questioning in the hand of God. There can be no greater warning and rebuke to those who work out dates and timetables as to when he will come again. Surely it is nothing less than blasphemy for us to enquire into that of which our Lord consented to be ignorant.

(iii) Jesus draws a practical conclusion. We are like men who know that their master will come, but who do not know when. We live in the shadow of eternity. That is no reason for fearful and hysterical expectation. But it means that day by day our work must be completed. It means that we must so live that it does not matter when he comes. It gives us the great task of making every day fit for him to see and being at any moment ready to meet him face to face. All life becomes a preparation to meet the King.

We began by saying that this was a very difficult chapter, but that in the end it had permanent truth to tell us.

(i) It tells us that only the man of God can see into the secrets of history. Jesus saw the fate of Jerusalem although others were blind to it. A real statesman must be a man of God. To guide his country a man must be himself God-guided. Only the man who knows God can enter into something of the plan of God.

(ii) It tells us two things about the doctrine of the Second Coming.

(*a*) It tells us that it contains a fact we forget or disregard at our peril.

(*b*) It tells us that the imagery in which it is clothed is the imagery of Jesus' own time, and that to speculate on it is useless, when Jesus himself was content not to know. The one thing of which we can be sure is that history is going somewhere; there is a consummation to come.

(iii) It tells us that of all things to forget God and to become immersed in earth is most foolish. The wise man is he who never forgets that he must be ready when the summons comes. If he lives in that memory, for him the end will not be terror, but eternal joy.

CHAPTER FOURTEEN

The Resurrection and the Life

John 11:20–27

When Martha met Jesus her heart spoke through her lips. Through the words we read her mind. Martha would have liked to say: "When you got our message, why didn't you come at once? And now you have left it too late." No sooner are the words out than there follow the words of faith, faith which defied the facts and defied experience: "Even yet," she said with a kind of desperate hope, "even yet, I know that God will give you whatever you ask."

Jesus said: "Your brother will rise again." Martha answered: "I know quite well that he will rise in the general resurrection on the last day." Now that is a notable saying. One of the strangest things in scripture is the fact that the saints of the Old Testament had practically no belief in any real life after death. In the early days, the Hebrews believed that the soul of every man, good and bad alike, went to Sheol. Sheol is wrongly translated *Hell;* for it was not a place of torture, it was the land of the shades. All alike went there and they lived a vague, shadowy, strengthless, joyless ghostly kind of life. This is the belief of by far the greater part of the Old Testament. "In death there is no remembrance of thee: in Sheol who can give thee praise?" (Psalm 6:5). "What profit is there in my death if I go down to the pit? Will the dust praise thee? Will it tell of thy faithfulness?" (Psalm 30:9). The Psalmist speaks of "the slain that lie in the grave, like those whom thou dost remember no more; for they are cut off from thy hand" (Psalm 88:5). "Is thy steadfast love declared in the grave," he asks, "or thy faithfulness in Abaddon? Are thy wonders known in the darkness, or thy saving help in the land of forgetfulness?" (Psalm 88:10–12). "The dead do not praise the Lord, nor do any that go down into silence" (Psalm 115:17). The preacher says grimly: "Whatever your hand finds to do, do it with your might; for there is no work or thought or knowledge or wisdom in Sheol, to which you are going" (Ecclesiastes 9:10). It is Hezekiah's pessimistic belief that: "For Sheol cannot thank thee, death cannot praise thee; those who go down to the pit cannot hope for thy faithfulness" (Isaiah 38:18). After death came the land of silence and of forgetfulness, where the shades of men were separated alike from men and from God.

Just very occasionally someone in the Old Testament made a venturesome leap of faith. The Psalmist cries: "My body also dwells secure. For thou dost not give me up to Sheol, or let thy godly one see the pit. Thou dost show me the path of life; in thy presence there is fullness of joy, in thy right hand are pleasures for evermore" (Psalm 16:9–11). "I am continually with thee; thou dost hold my right hand. Thou dost guide me with thy counsel, and afterward thou wilt receive me to glory" (Psalm 73:23, 24). The Psalmist was convinced that when a man entered into a real relationship with God, not even death could break it. But at that stage it was a desperate leap of faith rather than a settled conviction. Finally in the Old Testament there is the immortal hope we find in Job. In face of all his disasters Job cried out:

> I know that there liveth a champion,
> Who will one day stand over my dust;
> Yea, another shall rise as my witness,
> And, as sponsor, shall I behold God;
> Whom mine eyes shall behold, and no stranger's.
> (Job 14:7–12; translated by J. E. McFadyen)

Here in Job we have the real seed of the Jewish belief in immortality.

The Jewish history was a history of disasters, of captivity, slavery and defeat. Yet the Jewish people had the utterly unshakable conviction that they were God's own people. This earth had never shown it and never would; inevitably, therefore, they called in the new world to redress the inadequacies of the old. They came to see that if God's design was ever fully to be worked out, if his justice was ever completely to be fulfilled, if his love was ever finally to be satisfied, another world and another life were necessary. As Galloway (quoted by McFadyen) put it: "The enigmas of life become at least less baffling, when we come to rest in the thought that this is not the last act of the human drama." It was precisely that feeling that led the Hebrews to a conviction that there was a life to come.

It is true that in the days of Jesus the Sadducees still refused to believe in any life after death. But the Pharisees and the great majority of the Jews did. They said that in the moment of death the two worlds of time and of eternity met and kissed. They said that those who died beheld God, and they refused to call them the dead but called them the living. When Martha answered Jesus as she did she bore witness to the highest reach of her nation's faith.

Jesus brought into life the certainty that death is not the end. The last words of Edward the Confessor were: "Weep not, I shall not die; and as I leave the land of the dying I trust to see the blessings of the Lord in the land of the living." We call this world *the land of the living;* but it would in fact be more correct to call it *the land of the dying.* Through Jesus Christ we know that we are journeying, not to the sunset, but to the sunrise; we know, as Mary Webb put it, that death is a gate on the skyline. In the most real sense we are not on our way to death, but on our way to life.

CHAPTER FIFTEEN

Men under Judgment

Romans 14:10–12

The Roman well knew the sight of a man standing before the judge's judgment seat.

That is what happens to every man; and it is a judgment which he must face alone. Sometimes in this world he can make use of the merits of someone else. Many a young man has been spared some penalty for the sake of his parents; many a husband has been given mercy for the sake of his wife or child; but in the judgment of God a man stands alone. Sometimes, when a great one dies, the coffin lies in front of the mourning congregation, and, on the top of it, there is arranged the gowns of his academic honours, or the insignia of his state dignities; but he cannot take them with him. Naked we come into the world, and naked we leave it. We stand before God in the awful loneliness of our own souls; to him we can take nothing but the character which in life we have been building up.

Yet that is not the whole truth. We do not stand alone at the judgment seat of God, for we stand with Jesus Christ. We do not need to go stripped of everything; we may go clad in the merits that are his. Collin Brooks, writer and journalist, writes in one of his books: "God may be kinder than we think. If he cannot say, 'Well done! good and faithful servant,' it may be that he will say at last, 'Don't worry, my bad and faithless servant: I don't altogether dislike you.' " That was a man's whimsical way of stating his faith; but there is more to it than that. It is not that God merely does not dislike us; it is that, sinners as we are, he loves us for the sake of Jesus Christ. True, we must stand before God's judgment seat in the naked loneliness of our own souls; but, if we have lived with Christ in life, we shall stand with him in death, and before God he will be the advocate to plead our cause.

CHAPTER SIXTEEN

The Three Judgments

1 Corinthians 4:1–5

Paul speaks of three judgments that every man must face.

(i) He must face the judgment of his *fellowmen*. In this case Paul says that that is nothing to him. But there is a sense in which a man cannot disregard the judgment of his fellowmen. The odd thing is that, in spite of its occasional radical mistakes, the judgment of our fellowmen is often right. That is due to the fact that every man instinctively admires the basic qualities of honour, honesty, reliability, generosity, sacrifice and love. Antisthenes, the Cynic philosopher, used to say, "There are only two people who can tell you the truth about yourself—an enemy who has lost his temper and a friend who loves you dearly." It is quite true that we should never let the judgment of men deflect us from what we believe to be right; but it is also true that the judgment of men is often more accurate than we would like to think, because they instinctively admire the lovely things.

(ii) He must face the judgment of *himself*. Once again Paul disregards that. He knew very well that a man's judgment of himself can be clouded by self-satisfaction, by pride and by conceit. But in a very real sense every man must face his own judgment. One of the basic Greek ethical laws was, "Man, know thyself." The Cynics insisted that one of the first characteristics of a real man was "the ability to get on with himself." A man cannot get away from himself and if he loses his self-respect, life becomes an intolerable thing.

(iii) He must face the judgment of *God*. In the last analysis this is the only real judgment. For Paul, the judgment he awaited was not that of any human day but the judgment of the day of the Lord. God's is the final judgment for two reasons. (*a*) Only God knows all the *circumstances*. He knows the struggles a man has had; he knows the secrets that a man can tell to no one; he knows what a man might have sunk to and he also knows what he might have climbed to. (*b*) Only God knows all the *motives*. "Man sees the deed but God sees the intention." Many a deed that looks noble may have been done from the most selfish and ignoble motives; and many a deed which looks base may have been done from the highest motives. He who made the human heart alone knows it and can judge it.

We would do well to remember two things—first even if we escape all other judgments or shut our eyes to them, we cannot escape the judgment of God; and, second, judgment belongs to God and we do well not to judge any man.

CHAPTER SEVENTEEN

Jesus' Resurrection and Ours

1 Corinthians 15

First Corinthians 15 is both one of the greatest and one of the most difficult chapters in the New Testament. Not only is it in itself difficult, but it has also given to the creed a phrase which many people have grave difficulty in affirming, for it is from this chapter that we mainly derive the idea of *the resurrection of the body*. The chapter will be far less difficult if we study it against its background, and even that troublesome phrase will become quite clear and acceptable when we realize what Paul really meant by it. So then, before we study the chapter, there are certain things we would do well to have in mind.

(i) It is of great importance to remember that the Corinthians were denying not the Resurrection of Jesus Christ but the resurrection of the body; and what Paul was insistent upon was that if a man denied the resurrection of the body he thereby denied the Resurrection of Jesus Christ and therefore emptied the Christian message of its truth and the Christian life of its reality.

(ii) In any early Christian church there must have been two backgrounds, for in all churches there were Jews and Greeks.

First, there was the Jewish background. To the end of the day the Sadducees denied that there was any life after death at all. There was therefore one line of Jewish thought which completely denied both the immortality of the soul and the resurrection of the body (Acts 23:8). In the Old Testament there is very little hope of anything that can be called life after death. According to the general Old Testament belief all men, without distinction, went to Sheol after death. The Old

Testament is full of this bleak, grim pessimism regarding what is to happen after death.

> For in death there is no remembrance of thee: in Sheol who can give thee praise? (Psalm 6:5)

> What profit is there in my death if I go down to the pit? Will the dust praise thee? Will it tell of thy faithfulness? (Psalm 30:9)

> Dost thou work wonders for the dead? Do the shades rise up to praise thee? Is thy steadfast love declared in the grave? Or thy faithfulness in Abaddon? Are thy wonders known in the darkness, or thy saving help in the land of forgetfulness? (Psalm 88:10–12)

> The dead do not praise the Lord, nor do any that go down into silence. (Psalm 115:17)

> For Sheol cannot thank thee, death cannot praise thee; those who go down to the pit cannot hope for thy faithfulness. (Isaiah 38:18)

> Look away from me, that I may know gladness, before I depart and be no more. (Psalm 39:13)

> But he who is joined with all the living has hope; for a living dog is better than a dead lion. For the living know that they will die; but the dead know nothing. . . . Whatever your hand finds to do do it with your might; for there is no work, or thought, or knowledge, or wisdom, in Sheol to which you are going. (Ecclesiastes 9:4, 5, 10)

J. E. McFadyen, a great Old Testament scholar, says that this lack of a belief in immortality in the Old Testament is due "to the power with which those men apprehended God in this world." He goes on to say, "There are few more wonderful things than this in the long story of religion, that for centuries men lived the noblest lives, doing their duties and bearing their sorrows, without hope of future reward;

and they did this because in all their going out and coming in they were very sure of God."

It is true that in the Old Testament there are some few, some very few, glimpses of a real life to come. There were times when a man felt that, if God be God at all, there must be something which would reverse the incomprehensible verdicts of this world. So Job cries out,

> Still, I know One to champion me at last, to stand up for me upon earth. This body may break up, but even then my life shall have a sight of God. (Job 19:25–27, Moffatt)

The real feeling of the saint was that even in this life a man might enter into a relationship with God so close and so precious that not even death could break it.

> My body also dwells secure. For thou dost not give me up to Sheol, or let thy godly one see the Pit. Thou dost show me the path of life; in thy presence there is fulness of joy; in thy right hand there are pleasures for evermore.
>
> (Psalm 16:9–11)

> Thou dost hold my right hand. Thou dost guide me with thy counsel, and afterward thou wilt receive me to glory.
>
> (Psalm 73:24)

It is also true that in Israel the immortal hope developed. Two things helped that development. (*a*) Israel was the chosen people, and yet her history was one continued tale of disaster. Men began to feel that it required another world to redress the balance. (*b*) For many centuries it is true to say that the individual hardly existed. God was the God of the nation and the individual was an unimportant unit. But as the centuries went on religion became more and more personal. God became not the God of the nation but the friend of every individual; and so men began dimly and instinctively to feel that once a man knows God and is known by him, a relationship has been created which not even death can break.

(iii) When we turn to the Greek world, we must firmly grasp one thing, which is at the back of the whole chapter. The Greeks had an instinctive fear of death. Euripides wrote, "Yet mortals, burdened with countless ills, still love life. They long for each coming day, glad to bear the thing they know, rather than face death the unknown" (Fragment 813). But on the whole the Greeks, and that part of the world influenced by Greek thought, did believe in the immortality of the soul. But for them the immortality of the soul involved the complete dissolution of the body.

They had a proverb, "The body is a tomb." "I am a poor soul," said one of them, "shackled to a corpse." "It pleased me," said Seneca, "to enquire into the eternity of the soul—nay! to believe in it. I surrendered myself to that great hope." But he also says, "When the day shall come which shall part this mixture of divine and human, here where I found it, I will leave my body, myself I will give back to the gods." Epictetus writes, "When God does not supply what is necessary, he is sounding the signal for retreat—he has opened the door and says to you 'Come!' But whither? To nothing terrible, but to whence you came, to the things which are dear and kin to you, to the elements. What in you was fire shall go to fire, earth to earth, water to water." Seneca talks about things at death "being resolved into their ancient elements." For Plato "the body is the antithesis of the soul, as the source of all weaknesses as opposed to what alone is capable of independence and goodness." We can see this best in the Stoic belief. To the Stoic God was fiery spirit, purer than anything on earth. What gave men life was that a spark of this divine fire came and dwelt in a man's body. When a man died, his body simply dissolved into the elements of which it was made, but the divine spark returned to God and was absorbed in the divinity of which it was a part.

For the Greek immortality lay precisely in getting rid of the body. For him the resurrection of the body was unthinkable. Personal immortality did not really exist because that which gave men life was absorbed again in God the source of all life.

(iv) Paul's view was quite different. If we begin with one immense fact, the rest will become clear. The Christian belief is that after death individuality will survive, that you will still be you and I will still be I. Beside that we have to set another immense fact. To the Greek the body could not be consecrated. It was matter, the source of all evil, the prison-house of the soul. But to the Christian the body is not evil. Jesus, the Son of God, has taken this human body upon him and therefore it is not contemptible because it has been inhabited by God. To the Christian, therefore the life to come involves the total man, body and soul.

Now it is easy to misinterpret and to caricature the doctrine of the resurrection of the body. Celsus, who lived about A.D. 220, a bitter opponent of Christianity, did this very thing long ago. How can those who have died rise with their identical bodies? he demands. "Really it is the hope of worms! For what soul of a man would any longer wish for a body that had rotted?" It is easy to cite the case of a person smashed up in an accident or dying of cancer.

But Paul never said that we would rise with the body with which we died. He insisted that we would have a spiritual body. What he really meant was that a man's *personality* would survive. It is almost impossible to conceive of personality without a body, because it is through the body that the personality expresses itself. What Paul is contending for is that after death the individual remains. He did not inherit the Greek contempt of the body but believed in the resurrection of the whole man. He will still be himself; he will survive as a person. That is what Paul means by the resurrection of the body. Everything of the body and of the soul that is necessary to make a man a person will survive, but, at the same time, all things will be new, and body and spirit will alike be very different from earthly things, for they will alike be divine.

CHAPTER EIGHTEEN

The Physical and the Spiritual

1 Corinthians 15:35–49

Before we begin to try to interpret this section we would do well to remember one thing—all through it Paul is talking about things that no one really knows anything about. He is talking not about verifiable matters of fact, but about matters of faith. Trying to express the inexpressible and to describe the indescribable, he is doing the best he can with the human ideas and human words that are all that he has to work with. If we remember that, it will save us from a crudely literalistic interpretation and make us fasten our thoughts on the underlying principles in Paul's mind. In this section he is dealing with people who say, "Granted that there is a resurrection of the body, with what kind of body do people rise again?" His answer has three basic principles in it.

(i) He takes the analogy of a seed. The seed is put in the ground and dies, but in due time it rises again; and does so with a very different kind of body from that with which it was sown. Paul is showing that, at one and the same time, there can be dissolution, difference and yet continuity. The seed is dissolved; when it rises again, there is a vast difference in its body; and yet, in spite of the dissolution and the difference, it is the same seed. So our earthly bodies will dissolve; they will rise again in very different form; but it is the same person who rises. Dissolved by death, changed by resurrection, it is still we who exist.

(ii) In the world, even as we know it, there is not one kind of body; each separate part of creation has its own. God gives to each created thing a body suitable for its part in creation. If that be so, it is only reasonable to expect that he will give us a body fitted for the resurrection life.

(iii) In life there is a development. Adam, the first man, was made from the dust of the earth (Genesis 2:7). But Jesus is far more than a man made from the dust of the earth. He is the incarnation of the very Spirit of God. Now, under the old way of life, we were one with Adam, sharing his sin, inheriting his death and having his body; but, under the new way of life, we are one with Christ and we shall therefore share his life and his being. It is true that we have a physical body to begin with, but it is also true that one day we shall have a spiritual body.

All through this section Paul has maintained a reverent and wise reticence as to what that body will be like; it will be spiritual, it will be such as God knows that we need and we will be like Christ. But in verses 42–44 he draws four contrasts which shed light on our future state.

(i) The present body is corruptible; the future body will be incorruptible. In this world everything is subject to change and decay. "Youth's beauty fades, and manhood's glory fades," as Sophocles had it. But in the life to come there will be a permanence in which beauty will never lose its sheen.

(ii) The present body is in dishonour; the future body will be in glory. It may be that Paul means that in this life it is through our bodily feelings and passions that dishonour can so easily come; but in the life to come our bodies will no longer be the servants of passion and of impulse but the instruments of the pure service of God, than which there can be no greater honour.

(iii) The present body is in weakness; the future body will be in power. It is nowadays fashionable to talk of man's power, but the really remarkable thing is his weakness. A draught of air or a drop of water can kill him. We are limited in this life so often simply because of the necessary limitations of the body. Time and time again our physical constitution says to our visions and our plans, "Thus far and no farther." We are so often frustrated because we are what we are.

But in the life to come the limitations will be gone. Here we are compassed about with weakness; there we will be clad with power.

(iv) The present body is a natural body; the future body will be a spiritual body. By that, it may be, Paul meant that here we are but imperfect vessels and imperfect instruments for the Spirit; but in the life to come we will be such that the Spirit can truly fill us, as can never happen here, and the Spirit can truly use us, as is never possible now. Then we will be able to render the perfect worship, the perfect service, the perfect love that now can only be a vision and a dream.

CHAPTER NINETEEN

Joy and Judgment to Come

2 Corinthians 5:1–10

There is a very significant progression of thought in this passage, a progression which gives us the very essence of the thought of Paul.

(i) To him it will be a day of joy when he is done with this human body. He regards it as merely a tent, a temporary dwelling place, in which we sojourn till the day comes when it is dissolved and we enter into the real abode of our souls.

We have had occasion before to see how Greek and Roman thinkers despised the body. "The body," they said, "is a tomb." Plotinus could say that he was ashamed that he had a body. Epictetus said of himself, "Thou art a poor soul burdened with a corpse." Seneca wrote, "I am a higher being and born for higher things than to be the slave of my body which I look upon as only a shackle put upon my freedom. . . . In so detestable a habitation dwells the free soul." Even Jewish thought sometimes had this idea. "For the corruptible body presses down upon the soul and the earthly tabernacle weighs down the mind that muses on many things" (Wisdom 9:15).

With Paul there is a difference. He is not looking for a Nirvana with the peace of extinction; he is not looking for absorption in the divine; he is not looking for the freedom of a disembodied spirit; he is waiting for the day when God will give him a new body, a spiritual body, in which he will still be able, even in the heavenly places, to serve and to adore God. He saw eternity not as release into permanent inaction, but as the entry into a body in which service could be complete.

(ii) For all his yearning for the life to come, Paul does not despise this life. He is, says, in good heart. The reason is that even here and now we possess the Holy Spirit of God, and the Holy Spirit is the *arrabon* (cp. 1:22), the first installment of the life to come. It is Paul's conviction that already the Christian can enjoy the foretaste of the life everlasting. It is given to the Christian to be a citizen of two worlds; and the result is, not that he despises this world, but that he finds it clad with a sheen of glory which is the reflection of the greater glory to come.

(iii) Then comes the note of sternness. Even when Paul was thinking of the life to come, he never forgot that we are on the way not only to glory, but also to judgment. "We must all appear before the judgment seat of Christ."

Even so some day we shall await the verdict of God. When we remember that, life becomes a tremendous and a thrilling thing, for in it we are making or marring a destiny, winning or losing a crown. Time becomes the testing ground of eternity.

CHAPTER TWENTY

The Children of Light

Ephesians 5:9–14

Paul finishes this passage with a quotation in poetry. In Moffatt's translation it runs:

Wake up, O sleeper, and rise from the dead;
So Christ will shine upon you.

Paul introduces the quotation as if everybody knew it, but no one now knows where it came from. There are certain interesting suggestions.

Almost certainly, being in poetry, it is a fragment of an early Christian hymn. It may well have been part of a baptismal hymn. In the early church nearly all baptisms were of adults, confessing their faith as they came out of heathenism into Christianity. Perhaps these were the lines which were sung as they arose from the water, to symbolize the passage from the dark sleep of paganism to the awakened life of the Christian way.

Again, it has been suggested that these lines are part of a hymn, which was supposed to give the summons of the archangel when the last trumpet sounded over the earth. Then would be the great awakening when men rose from the sleep of death to receive the eternal life of Christ.

These things are speculations, but it seems certain that when we read these lines, we are reading a fragment of one of the first hymns the Christian church ever sang.

CHAPTER TWENTY-ONE

Those Who Are Asleep

1 Thessalonians 4:13–18

The idea of the Second Coming had brought another problem to the people of Thessalonica. They were expecting it very soon; they fully expected to be themselves alive when it came but they were worried about those Christians who had died. They could not be sure that those who had already died would share the glory of that day which was so soon to come. Paul's answer is that there will be one glory for those who have died and those who survive.

He tells them that they must not sorrow as those who have no hope. In face of death the pagan world stood in despair. They met it with grim resignation and bleak hopelessness.

Paul lays down a great principle. The man who has lived and died in Christ is still in Christ even in death and will rise in him. Between Christ and the man who loves him there is a relationship which nothing can break, a relationship which overpasses death. Because Christ died and rose again, so the man who is one with Christ will rise again.

The picture Paul draws of the day when Christ will come is poetry, an attempt to describe what is indescribable. At the Second Coming Christ will descend from heaven to earth. He will utter the word of command and thereupon the voice of an archangel and the trumpet of God will waken the dead; then the dead and the living alike will be caught up in the chariots of the clouds to meet Christ; and thereafter they will be forever with their Lord. We are not meant to take with crude and insensitive literalism what is a seer's vision. It is not the details which are important. What is important is that in life and in death the Christian is in Christ and that is a union which nothing can break.

CHAPTER TWENTY-TWO

Like a Thief in the Night

1 Thessalonians 5:1–11

Very naturally the New Testament writers to all intents and purposes identified the day of the Lord with the day of the Second Coming of Jesus Christ. We will do well to remember that these are what we might call stock pictures. They are not meant to be taken literally. They are pictorial visions of what would happen when God broke into time.

Naturally men were anxious to know when that day would come. Jesus himself had bluntly said that no man knew when that day or hour would be, that even he did not know and only God knew (Mark 13:32; cp. Matthew 24:36; Acts 1:7). But that did not stop people speculating about it, as indeed they still do, although it is surely almost blasphemous that men should seek for knowledge which was denied even to Jesus. To these speculations Paul has two things to say.

He repeats that the coming of the day will be sudden. It will come like a thief in the night. But he also insists that that is no reason why a man should be caught unawares. It is only the man who lives in the dark and whose deeds are evil who will be caught unprepared. The Christian lives in the light and no matter when that day comes, if he is watchful and sober, it will find him ready. Waking or sleeping, the Christian is living already with Christ and is therefore always prepared.

No man knows when God's call will come for him and there are certain things that cannot be left until the last moment. It is too late to prepare for an examination when the examination paper is before you. It is too late to make the house secure when the storm has burst. If a call comes suddenly, it need not find us unprepared. The man who has lived all his life with Christ is never unprepared to enter his nearer presence.

CHAPTER TWENTY-THREE

The Lawless One

2 Thessalonians 2:1–12

Paul was telling the Thessalonians that they must give up their nervous, hysterical waiting for the Second Coming. He denied that he had ever said that the day of the Lord had come. That was a misinterpretation of his words which must not be attributed to him; and he told them that before the day of the Lord could come much had still to happen.

First there would come an age of rebellion against God; into this world there had already come a secret evil power which was working in the world and on men to bring this time of rebellion. Somewhere there was being kept one who was as much the incarnation of evil as Jesus was the incarnation of God. He was The Man of Sin, The Son of Perdition, The Lawless One. In time the power which was restraining him would be removed from the scene; and then this devil incarnate would come. When he came, he would gather his own people to him just as Jesus Christ had gathered his. Those who had refused to accept Christ were waiting to accept him. Then would come a last battle in which Christ would utterly destroy The Lawless One; Christ's people would be gathered to him and the wicked men who had accepted The Lawless One as their master would be destroyed.

We have to remember one thing. Almost all the Eastern faiths believed in a power of evil as they believed in a power of good; and believed, too, in a kind of battle between God and this power of evil. The Jews, too, had that idea. They called the Satanic power *Belial* or, more correctly, *Beliar.* When the Jews wished to describe a man as utterly bad they called him *a son of Beliar* (Deuteronomy 13:13; 1 Kings 21:10, 13; 2 Samuel 22:5). In 2 Corinthians 6:15 Paul uses this term as the opposite of God. This evil incarnate was the antithesis of God. The Christians took this over, later than Paul, under the title *Antichrist* (1 John 2:18, 22; 4:3). Obviously such a power cannot go on existing for ever in the universe; and there was widespread belief in a final battle in which God would triumph and this force of anti-God would be finally destroyed. That is the picture with which Paul is working.

What was the restraining force which was still keeping The Lawless One under control? No one can answer that question with certainty. Most likely Paul meant the Roman Empire. Time and again he himself was to be saved from the fury of the mob by the justice of the Roman magistrate. Rome was the restraining power which kept the world from insane anarchy. But the day would come when that power would be removed—and then would be chaos.

So then Paul pictures a growing rebellion against God, the emergence of one who was the devil incarnate as Christ had been God incarnate, a final struggle and the ultimate triumph of God.

When this incarnate evil came into the world there would be some who would accept him as master, those who had refused Christ; and they along with their evil master would find final defeat and terrible judgment.

However remote these pictures may be from us they nevertheless have certain permanent truth in them.

(i) There is a force of evil in the world. Even if he could not logically prove that there was a devil many a man would say, "I know there is because I have met him." We hide our heads in the sand if we deny that there is an evil power at work amongst men.

(ii) God is in control. Things may seem to be crashing to chaos but in some strange way even the chaos is in God's control.

(iii) The ultimate triumph of God is sure. In the end nothing can stand against him. The Lawless One may have his day but there comes a time when God says, "Thus far and no farther." And so the great question is, "On what side are you? In the struggle at the heart of the universe are you for God—or Satan?"

CHAPTER TWENTY-FOUR

Times of Terror

2 Timothy 3:1

It is in terms of the last days that Paul is thinking in this passage.

He says that in them *difficult* times would set in. *Difficult* is the Greek word *chalepos*. It is the normal Greek word for *difficult,* but it has certain usages which explain its meaning here. It is used in Matthew 8:28 to describe the two Gergesene demoniacs who met Jesus among the tombs. They were violent and dangerous. It is used in Plutarch to describe what we would call an *ugly* wound. It is used by ancient writers on astrology to describe what we would call a *threatening* conjunction of the heavenly bodies. There is the idea of menace and of danger in this word. In the last days there would come times which would menace the very existence of the Christian church and of goodness itself, a kind of last tremendous assault of evil before its final defeat.

In the Jewish pictures of these last terrible times we get exactly the same kind of picture as we get here. There would come a kind of terrible flowering of evil, when the moral foundations seemed to be shaken. In the *Testament of Issachar,* one of the books written between the Old and the New Testaments, we get a picture like this:

> Know ye, therefore, my children, that in the last times
> Your sons will forsake singleness
> And will cleave unto insatiable desire;
> And leaving guilelessness, will draw near to malice;
> And forsaking the commandments of the Lord,

They will cleave unto Beliar.
And leaving husbandry,
They will follow after their own wicked devices,
And they shall be dispersed among the Gentiles,
And shall serve their enemies.

                          (*Testament of Issachar* 6:1, 2)

In this picture which Paul draws he is thinking in terms familiar to the Jews. There was to be a final showdown with the forces of evil.

Nowadays we have to restate these old pictures in modern terms. They were never meant to be anything else but visions; we do violence to Jewish and to early Christian thought if we take them with a crude literalness. But they do enshrine the permanent truth that some time there must come the consummation when evil meets God in head-on collision and there comes the final triumph of God.

CHAPTER TWENTY-FIVE

The Perfect Purification

Hebrews 9:23–28

The writer to the Hebrews draws a parallel between the life of man and the life of Christ.

(i) Man dies and then comes the judgment. That itself was a shock to the Greek for he tended to believe that death was final. The significant thing about this passage of Hebrews is its basic assumption that a man will rise again. That is part of the certainty of the Christian creed; and the basic warning is that he rises to judgment.

(ii) With Christ it is different—he dies and rises and comes again, and he comes not to be judged but to judge. The early church never forgot the hope of the Second Coming. It throbbed through their belief. But for the unbeliever that was a day of terror. In some way the consummation must come. If in that day Christ comes as a friend, it can be only a day of glory; if he comes as a stranger or as one whom we have regarded as an enemy, it can be only a day of judgment. A man may look to the end of things with joyous expectation or with shuddering terror. What makes the difference is how his heart is with Christ.

CHAPTER TWENTY-SIX

The Second Coming

1 Peter

When we go to the letter we find that expectation of the Second Coming of Christ is in the very forefront of its thought. Christians are being kept for the salvation which is to be revealed at the last time (1:5). Those who keep the faith will be saved from the coming judgment (1:7). Christians are to hope for the grace which will come at the revelation of Jesus Christ (1:13). The day of visitation is expected (2:12). The end of all things is at hand (4:7). Those who suffer with Christ will also rejoice with Christ when his glory is revealed (4:13). Judgment is to begin at the house of God (4:17). The writer himself is sure that he will be a sharer in the glory to come (5:1). When the Chief Shepherd shall appear the faithful Christian will receive a crown of glory (5:4).

From beginning to end of the letter the Second Coming is in the forefront of the writer's mind. It is the motive for steadfastness in the faith, for the loyal living of the Christian life and for gallant endurance amidst the sufferings which have come and will come upon them.

It would be untrue to say that the Second Coming ever dropped out of Christian belief, but it did recede from the forefront of Christian belief as the years passed on and Christ did not return. It is, for instance, significant that in Ephesians, one of Paul's latest letters, there is no mention of it. On this ground it is reasonable to suppose that 1 Peter is early and comes from the days when the Christians vividly expected the return of their Lord at any moment.

CHAPTER TWENTY-SEVEN

The Approaching End

1 Peter 4:7

Here is a note which is struck consistently all through the New Testament. It is the summons of Paul that it is time to wake out of sleep, for the night is far spent and the day is at hand (Romans 13:12). "The Lord is at hand," he writes to the Philippians (Philippians 4:5). "The coming of the Lord is at hand," writes James (James 5:8). John says that the days in which his people are living are the last hour (1 John 2:18). "The time is near," says the John of the Revelation, and he hears the Risen Christ testify: "Surely I am coming soon" (Revelation 1:3; 22:20).

There are many for whom all such passages are problems, for, if they are taken literally, the New Testament writers were mistaken; nineteen hundred years have passed and the end is not yet come. There are four ways of looking at them.

(i) We may hold that the New Testament writers were in fact mistaken. They looked for the return of Christ and the end of the world in their own day and generation; and these events did not take place. The curious thing is that the Christian church allowed these words to stand although it would not have been difficult quietly to excise them from the New Testament documents. It was not until late in the second century that the New Testament began to be fixed in the form in which we have it today; and yet statements such as these became unquestioned parts of it. The clear conclusion is that the people of the early church still believed these words to be true.

(ii) There is a strong line of New Testament thought which in effect, holds that the end *has* come. The consummation of history was the coming of Jesus Christ. In him time was invaded by eternity. In him God entered into the human situation. In him the prophecies were all fulfilled. In him the end has come. Paul speaks of himself and his people as those on whom the ends of the ages have come (1 Corinthians 10:11). Peter in his first sermon speaks of Joel's prophecy of the outpouring of the spirit and of all that should happen in the last days, and then says that at that very time men were actually living in those last days (Acts 2:16–21).

If we accept that, it means that in Jesus Christ the end of history has come. The battle has been won; there remain only skirmishes with the last remnants of opposition. It means that at this very moment we are living in the "end time," in what someone has called "the epilogue to history." That is a very common point of view; but the trouble is that it flies in the face of facts. Evil is as rampant as ever; the world is still far from having accepted Christ as King. It may be the "end time," but the dawn seems as far distant as ever it was.

(iii) It may be that we have to interpret *near* in the light of history's being a process of almost unimaginable length. It has been put this way. Suppose all time to be represented by a column the height of Cleopatra's Needle with a single postage stamp on top, then the length of recorded history is represented by the thickness of the postage stamp and the unrecorded history which went before it by the height of the column. When we think of time in terms like that *near* becomes an entirely relative word. The Psalmist was literally right when he said that in God's sight a thousand years were just like a watch in the night (Psalm 90:4). In that case *near* can cover centuries and still be correctly used. But it is quite certain that the biblical writers did not take *near* in that sense, for they had no conception of history in terms like that.

(iv) The simple fact is that behind this there is one inescapable and most personal truth. *For everyone of us the time is near.* The one thing which can be said of every man is that he will die. For every one of us the Lord is at hand. We cannot tell the day and the hour when we shall go to meet him; and, therefore, all life is lived in the shadow of eternity.

"The end of all things is near," said Peter. The early thinkers may have been wrong if they thought that the end of the world was round the corner, but they have left us with the warning that for every one of us personally the end is near; and that warning is as valid today as ever it was.

CHAPTER TWENTY-EIGHT

The Message

2 Peter 1:16–18

Peter comes to the message which it was his great aim to bring to his people, concerning "the power and the coming of our Lord Jesus Christ." As we shall see quite clearly as we go on, the great aim of this letter is to recall men to certainty in regard to the Second Coming of Jesus Christ. The heretics whom Peter is attacking no longer believed in it; it was so long delayed that people had begun to think it would never happen at all.

Such, then, was Peter's message. Having stated it, he goes on to speak of his right to state it; and does something which is, at least at first sight, surprising. His right to speak is that he was with Jesus on the Mount of Transfiguration and that there he saw the glory and the honour which were given to him and heard the voice of God speak to him. That is to say, Peter uses the transfiguration story, not as a foretaste of the Resurrection of Jesus, as it is commonly regarded, but as a foretaste of the triumphant glory of the Second Coming. The transfiguration story is told in Matthew 17:1–8; Mark 9:2–8; Luke 9:28–36. Was Peter right in seeing in it a foretaste of the Second Coming rather than a prefiguring of the Resurrection?

There is one particularly significant thing about the transfiguration story. In all three Gospels, it immediately follows the prophecy of Jesus which said that there were some standing there who would not pass from the world until they had seen the Son of Man coming in his kingdom (Matthew 16:29; Mark 9:1; Luke 9:27). That would certainly seem to indicate that the transfiguration and the Second Coming were in some way linked together.

Whatever we may say, this much is certain, that Peter's great aim in this letter is to recall his people to a living belief in the Second Coming of Christ and he bases his right to do so on what he saw on the Mount of Transfiguration.

In verse 16 there is a very interesting word. Peter says, "We were made *eye-witnesses* of his majesty." The word he uses for *eye-witness* is *epoptes*. In the Greek usage of Peter's day this was a technical word. The Mystery Religions were all of the nature of passion plays, in which the story of a god who lived, suffered, died, and rose again was played out. It was only after a long course of instruction and preparation that the worshipper was finally allowed to be present at the passion play, and to be offered the experience of becoming one with the dying and rising God. When he reached this stage, he was an initiate and the technical word to describe him was *epoptes;* he was a privileged eye-witness of the experiences of God. So Peter says that the Christian is an eye-witness of the sufferings of Christ. With the eye of faith he sees the cross; in the experience of faith he dies with Christ to sin and rises to righteousness. His faith has made him one with Jesus Christ in his death and in his risen life and power.

CHAPTER TWENTY-NINE

Denial of the Second Coming

2 Peter 3:3–4

The argument of Peter's opponents was twofold (verse 4). "What has happened," they demanded, "to the promise of the Second Coming?" Their first argument was that the promise had been so long delayed that it was safe to take it that it would never be fulfilled. Their second assertion was that their fathers had died and the world was going on precisely as it always did. Their argument was that this was characteristically a stable universe and convulsive upheavals like the Second Coming did not happen in such a universe.

Peter's response is also twofold. He deals with the second argument first (verses 5–7). His argument is that, in fact, this is not a stable universe, that once it was destroyed by water in the time of the Flood and that a second destruction, this time by fire, is on the way.

The second part of his reply is in verses 8 and 9. His opponents speak of a delay so long that they can safely assume that the Second Coming is not going to happen at all. Peter's is a double answer. (*a*) We must see time as God sees it. With him a day is as a thousand years and a thousand years as a day. "God does not pay every Friday night." (*b*) In any event God's apparent slowness to act is not dilatoriness. It is, in fact, mercy. He holds his hand in order to give sinning men another chance to repent and find salvation.

Peter goes on to his conclusion (verse 10). The Second Coming is on the way and it will come with a sudden terror and destruction which will dissolve the universe in melting heat. Finally comes his practical demand in face of all this. If we are living in a universe on which Jesus Christ is going to descend and which is hastening towards the destruction of the wicked, surely it behoves us to live in holiness so that we may be spared when the terrible day does come. The Second Coming is used as a tremendous motive for moral amendment so that a man may prepare himself to meet his God.

CHAPTER THIRTY

The Dreadful Day

2 Peter 3:10

What Peter and many of the New Testament writers did was to identify the Old Testament pictures of the day of the Lord with the New Testament conception of the Second Coming of Jesus Christ. Peter's picture here of the Second Coming of Jesus is drawn in terms of the Old Testament picture of the day of the Lord.

He uses one very vivid phrase. He says that the heavens will pass away with a cracking roar (*roizedon*). The word is used for the whirring of a bird's wings in the air, for the sound a spear makes as it hurtles through the air, for the cracking of the flames of a forest fire.

We need not take these pictures with crude literalism. It is enough to note that Peter sees the Second Coming as a time of terror for those who are the enemies of Christ.

One thing has to be held in the memory. The whole conception of the Second Coming is full of difficulty. But this is sure—there comes a day when God breaks into every life, for there comes a day when we must die; and for that day we must be prepared. We may say what we will about the coming of Christ as a future event; we may feel it is a doctrine we have to lay on one side; but we cannot escape from the certainty of the entry of God into our own experience.

CHAPTER THIRTY-ONE

Hastening the Day

2 Peter 3:11–14

There is in this passage a great conception. Peter speaks of the Christian as not only eagerly awaiting the coming of Christ but as actually hastening it on. The New Testament tells us certain ways in which this may be done.

(i) It may be done by *prayer*. Jesus taught us to pray: "Thy Kingdom come" (Matthew 6:10). The earnest prayer of the Christian heart hastens the coming of the King. If in no other way, it does so in this—that he who prays opens his own heart for the entry of the King.

(ii) It may be done by *preaching*. Matthew tells us that Jesus said, "And this gospel of the Kingdom will be preached throughout the whole world, as a testimony to all nations; and then the end will come" (Matthew 24:14). All men must be given the chance to know and to love Jesus Christ before the end of creation is reached. The missionary activity of the church is the hastening of the coming of the King.

(iii) It may be done by *penitence* and *obedience*. Of all things this would be nearest to Peter's mind and heart. The rabbis had two sayings: "It is the sins of the people which prevent the coming of the Messiah. If the Jews would genuinely repent for one day, the Messiah would come." The other form of the saying means the same: "If Israel would perfectly keep the law for one day, the Messiah would come." In true penitence and in real obedience a man opens his own heart to the coming of the King and brings nearer that coming throughout the world. We do well to remember that our coldness of heart and our disobedience delay the coming of the King.

CHAPTER THIRTY-TWO

The Last Days, the Last Hour

1 John 2:18

It is important that we should understand what John means when he speaks of the time of the last hour. The idea of the last days and of the last hour runs all through the Bible; but there is a most interesting development in its meaning.

(i) The phrase occurs frequently in the very early books of the Old Testament. Jacob, for instance, before his death assembles his sons to tell them what will befall them in the last days (Genesis 49:1; cp. Numbers 24:14). At that time the last days were when the people of Israel would enter into the Promised Land, and would at last enter into full enjoyment of the promised blessings of God.

(ii) The phrase frequently occurs in the prophets. In the last days the mountain of the Lord shall be established as the highest of the mountains, and shall be raised above the hills, and all nations shall flow to it (Isaiah 2:2; Micah 4:1). In the last days God's Holy City will be supreme; and Israel will render to God the perfect obedience which is his due (cp. Jeremiah 23:20; 30:24; 48:47). In the last days there will be the supremacy of God and the obedience of his people.

(iii) In the Old Testament itself, and in the times between the Old and the New Testaments, the last days become associated with the day of the Lord. No conception is more deeply interwoven into scripture than this. The Jews had come to believe that all time was divided into two ages. In between *this present age,* which was wholly evil, and *the age to come,* which was the golden time of God's supremacy, there was the day of the Lord, the last days, which would be a time of terror, of cosmic dissolution and of judgment, the birth-pangs of the new age.

The last hour does not mean a time of annihilation whose end will be a great nothingness as there was at the beginning. In biblical thought the last time is the end of one age and the beginning of another. It is *last* in the sense that things as they are pass away; but it leads not to world obliteration but to world re-creation.

Here is the centre of the matter. The question then becomes: "Will a man be wiped out in the judgment of the old or will he enter into the glory of the new?" That is the alternative with which John—like all the biblical writers—is confronting men. Men have the choice of allying themselves with the old world, which is doomed to dissolution, or of allying themselves with Christ and entering into the new world, the very world of God. Here lies the urgency. If it was a simple matter of utter obliteration, no one could do anything about it. But it is a matter of re-creation, and whether a man will enter the new world or not depends on whether or not he gives his life to Jesus Christ.

In fact John was wrong. It was not the last hour for his people. Eighteen hundred years have gone by and the world still exists. Does the whole conception, then, belong to a sphere of thought which must be discarded? The answer is that in this conception there is an eternal relevance. *Every hour is the last hour.* In the world there is a continual conflict between good and evil, between God and that which is anti-God. And in every moment and in every decision a man is confronted with the choice of allying himself either with God or with the evil forces which are against God; and of thereby ensuring, or failing to ensure, his own share in eternal life. The conflict between good and evil never stops; therefore, the choice never stops; therefore, in a very real sense every hour is the last hour.

CHAPTER THIRTY-THREE

The Antichrist

1 and 2 John

In this verse we meet the conception of *Antichrist. Antichrist* is a word which occurs only in John's letters in the New Testament (1 John 2:22; 4:3; 2 John 7); but it is the expression of an idea which is as old as religion itself.

From its derivation *Antichrist* can have two meanings. *Anti* is a Greek preposition which can mean either *against* or *in place of. Strategos* is the Greek word for a *commander,* and *antistrategos* can mean either the *hostile commander* or the *deputy commander. Antichrist* can mean either the opponent of Christ or the one who seeks to put himself in the place of Christ. In this case the meaning will come to the same thing, but with this difference. If we take the meaning to be *the one who is opposed to Christ,* the opposition is plain. If we take the meaning to be *the one who seeks to put himself in the place of Christ,* Antichrist can be one who subtly tries to take the place of Christ from within the church and the Christian community. The one will be an open opposition; the other a subtle infiltration. We need not choose between these meanings, for Antichrist can act in either way.

The simplest way to think of it is that Christ is the incarnation of God and goodness, and Antichrist is the incarnation of the devil and evil.

We began by saying that this is an idea which is as old as religion itself; men have always felt that in the universe there is a power which is in opposition to God. One of its earliest forms occurs in the Babylonian legend of creation. According to it there was in the very beginning a primaeval sea monster called Tiamat; this sea monster was subdued by Marduk but not killed; it was only asleep and the final battle was still to come. That mythical idea of the primaeval monster occurs in the Old Testament again and again. There the monster is often called Rahab or the crooked serpent or leviathan. "Thou didst crush Rahab like a carcass," says the Psalmist (Psalm 89:10). "His hand pierced the fleeing serpent," says Job (Job 26:13). Isaiah, speaking of the arm of the Lord, says, "Was it not thou that didst cut Rahab in pieces, that didst pierce the dragon?" (Isaiah 51:9). Isaiah writes: "In that day the Lord with his hard and great and strong sword will punish leviathan the fleeing serpent, leviathan the twisting serpent, and he will slay the dragon that is in the sea" (Isaiah 27:1). All these are references to the primaeval dragon. This idea is obviously one which belongs to the childhood of mankind and its basis is that in the universe there is a power hostile to God.

Originally this power was conceived of as the dragon. Inevitably as time went on it became personalized. Every time there arose a very evil man who seemed to be setting himself against God and bent on the obliteration of his people, the tendency was to identify him with this anti-God force. For instance, about 168 B.C. there emerged the figure of Antiochus Epiphanes, King of Syria. He resolved on a deliberate attempt to eliminate Judaism from this earth. He invaded Jerusalem, killed thousands of Jews, and sold tens of thousands into slavery. To circumcise a child or to own a copy of the Law was made a crime punishable by instant death. In the Temple courts was erected a great altar to Zeus. Swine's flesh was offered on it. The Temple chambers were made into public brothels. Here was a cold-blooded effort to wipe out the Jewish religion. It was Antiochus whom Daniel called "the abomination that makes desolate" (Daniel 11:31; 12:11). Here men thought was the anti-God force become flesh.

It was this same phrase that men took in the days of Mark's Gospel when they talked of "The Abomination of Desolation"—"The Appalling Horror," as Moffatt translates it—being set up in the Temple (Mark 13:14; Matthew 24:15). Here the reference was to Caligula, the more than half-mad Roman Emperor, who wished to set up his own image in the Holy of Holies in the Temple. It was felt that this was the act of anti-God incarnate.

In 2 Thessalonians 2:3, 4, Paul speaks of "the man of sin," the one who exalts himself above all that is called God and all that is worshipped and who sets himself up in the very Temple of God. We do not know whom Paul was expecting, but again there is this thought of one who was the incarnation of everything which was opposed to God.

In Revelation there is the beast (13:1; 16:13; 19:20; 20:10). Here is very probably another figure. Nero was regarded by all as a human monster. His excesses disgusted the Romans and his savage persecution tortured the Christians. In due time he died; but he had been so wicked that men could not believe that he was really dead. And so there arose the *Nero redivivus,* Nero resurrected, legend, which said that Nero was not dead but had gone to Parthia and would come with the Parthian hordes to descend upon men. He is the beast, the Antichrist, the incarnation of evil.

All down history there have been these identifications of human figures with Antichrist. The Pope, Napoleon, Mussolini, Hitler, have all in their day received this identification.

But the fact is that Antichrist is not so much a person as a principle, the principle which is actively opposed to God and which may well be thought of as incarnating itself in those men in every generation who have seemed to be the blatant opponents of God.

John has a view of Antichrist which is characteristically his own. To him the sign that Antichrist is in the world is the false belief and the dangerous teaching of the heretics. The Church had been well forewarned that in the last days false teachers would come. Jesus had said, "Many will come in my name, saying, I am he; and they will lead many astray" (Mark 13:6; cp. Matthew 24:5). Before he left them, Paul had warned his Ephesian friends: "After my departure fierce wolves will come in among you, not sparing the flock. And from among your own selves will arise men, speaking perverse things, to draw away the disciples after them" (Acts 20:29, 30). The situation which had been foretold had now arisen.

But John had a special view of this situation. He did not think of Antichrist as one single individual figure but rather as a power of falsehood speaking in and through the false teachers. Just as the Holy Spirit was inspiring the true teachers and the true prophets, so there was an evil spirit inspiring the false teachers and the false prophets.

The great interest and relevance of this is that for John *the battleground was in the mind.* The spirit of Antichrist was struggling with the Spirit of God for the possession of men's minds. What makes this so significant is that we can see exactly this process at work today. Men have brought the indoctrination of the human mind to a science. We see men take an idea and repeat it and repeat it and repeat it until it settles into the minds of others and they begin to accept it as true simply because they have heard it so often. This is easier today than ever it was with so many means of mass communication—books, newspapers, wireless, television, and the vast resources of modern advertising. A skilled propagandist can take an idea and infiltrate it into men's minds until, all unaware, they are indoctrinated with it. We do not say that John foresaw all this but he did see the mind as the field of operations for Antichrist. He no longer thought in terms of a single demonic figure but in terms of a force of evil deliberately seeking to pervade men's minds; and there is nothing more potent for evil than that.

CHAPTER THIRTY-FOUR

Apocalyptic Literature

[From Barclay's introduction to Revelation]

In any study of the Revelation we must begin by remembering the basic fact that although unique in the New Testament, it is nonetheless representative of a kind of literature which was the commonest of all between the Old and the New Testaments. The Revelation is commonly called the Apocalypse, being in Greek *Apokalupsis*. Between the Old and the New Testaments there grew up a great mass of what is called *apocalyptic literature,* the product of an indestructible Jewish hope.

The Jews could not forget that they were the chosen people of God. To them that involved the certainty that some day they would arrive at world supremacy. In their early history they looked forward to the coming of a king of David's line who would unite the nation and lead them to greatness.

But the whole history of Israel gave the lie to these hopes. After the death of Solomon, the kingdom, small enough to begin with, split into two under Rehoboam and Jeroboam and so lost its unity. The northern kingdom, with its capital at Samaria, vanished in the last quarter of the eighth century B.C. before the assault of the Assyrians, never again reappeared in history and is now the lost ten tribes. The southern kingdom, with its capital at Jerusalem, was reduced to slavery and exile by the Babylonians in the early part of the sixth century B.C. It was later the subject state of the Persians, the Greeks and the Romans. History for the Jews was a catalogue of disasters from which it became clear that no human deliverer could rescue them.

1. The Two Ages

Jewish thought stubbornly held to the conviction of the chosenness of the Jews but had to adjust itself to the facts of history. It did so by working out a scheme of history. The Jews divided all time into two ages. There was *this present age,* which is wholly bad and beyond redemption. For it there can be nothing but total destruction. The Jews, therefore, waited for the end of things as they are. There was *the age which is to come* which was to be wholly good, the golden age of God in which would be peace, prosperity and righteousness and God's chosen people would at last be vindicated and receive the place that was theirs by right.

How was this present age to become the age which is to come? The Jews believed that the change could never be brought about by human agency and, therefore, looked for the direct intervention of God. He would come striding on to the stage of history to blast this present world out of existence and bring in his golden time. The day of the coming of God was called *the day of the Lord* and was to be a terrible time of terror and destruction and judgment which would be the birthpangs of the new age.

All apocalyptic literature deals with these events, the sin of the present age, the terrors of the time between, and the blessings of the time to come. It is entirely composed of dreams and visions of the end. That means that all apocalyptic literature is necessarily cryptic. It is continually attempting to describe the indescribable, to say the unsayable, to paint the unpaintable.

This is further complicated by another fact. It was only natural that these apocalyptic visions should flame the more brightly in the minds of men living under tyranny and oppression. The more some alien power held them down, the more they dreamed of the destruction of that power and of their own vindication. But it would only have worsened the situation, if the oppressing power could have understood these dreams. Such writings would have seemed the works of rebellious revolutionaries. Such books, therefore, were frequently written in code, deliberately couched in language which was unintelligible to the outsider; and there are many cases in which they must remain unintelligible because the key to the code no longer exists. But the more we know about the historical background of such books, the better we can interpret them.

All this is the precise picture of our Revelation. There are any number of Jewish apocalypses—*Enoch,* the *Sibylline Oracles,* the *Testaments of the Twelve Patriarchs,* the *Ascension of Isaiah,* the *Assumption of Moses,* the *Apocalypse of Baruch,* 4 Ezra. Our Revelation is a Christian apocalypse. It is the only one in the New Testament, although there were many others which did not gain admission. It is written exactly on the Jewish pattern and follows the basic conception of the two ages. The only difference is that for the day of the Lord it substitutes the coming in power of Jesus Christ. Not only the pattern but the details are the same. The Jewish apocalypses had a standard apparatus of events which were to happen at the last time; these events all have their place in Revelation.

Before we go on to outline that pattern of events, another question arises. Both *apocalyptic* and *prophecy* deal with the events which are to come. What, then, is the difference between them?

2. Apocalyptic and Prophecy

The difference between the prophets and the apocalyptists was very real. There were two main differences, one of message and one of method.

(i) The prophet thought in terms of this present world. His message was often a cry for social, economic and political justice; and was always a summons to obey and serve God within this present world. To the prophet it was this world which was to be reformed and in which God's kingdom would come. This has been expressed by saying that the prophet believed in history. He believed that in the events of history God's purpose was being worked out. In one sense the prophet was an optimist, for, however sternly he condemned things as they were, he nonetheless believed that they could be mended, if men would accept the will of God. To the apocalyptist the world was beyond mending. He believed, not in the reformation, but in the dissolution of this present world. He looked forward to the creation of a new world, when this one had been shattered by the avenging wrath of God. In one sense, therefore, the apocalyptist was a pessimist, for he did not believe that things as they were could ever be cured. True, he was quite certain that the golden age would come, but only after this world had been destroyed.

(ii) The prophet's message was spoken; the message of the apocalyptist was always written. Apocalyptic is a literary production. Had it been delivered by word of mouth, men would never have understood it. It is difficult, involved, often unintelligible; it has to be pored over before it can be understood. Further, the prophet always spoke under his own name; all apocalyptic writings—except our New Testament one—are pseudonymous. They are put into the mouths of great ones of the past, like Noah, Enoch, Isaiah, Moses, the Twelve Patriarchs, Ezra and Baruch. There is something pathetic about this. The men who wrote the apocalyptic literature had the feeling that greatness was gone from the earth; they were too self-distrusting to put their names to their works and attributed them to the great figures of the past, thereby seeking to give them an authority greater than their own names could have given. As Julicher put it: "Apocalyptic is prophecy turned senile."

3. The Apparatus of Apocalyptic

Apocalyptic literature has a pattern; it seeks to describe the things which will happen at the last times and the blessedness which will follow; and the same pictures occur over and over again. It always, so to speak, worked with the same materials; and these materials find their place in our Book of the Revelation.

(i) In apocalyptic literature the Messiah was a divine, pre-existent, otherworldly figure of power and glory, waiting to descend into the world to begin his all-conquering career. He existed in heaven before the creation of the world, before the sun and the stars were made, and he is preserved in the presence of the Almighty (*Enoch* 48:3, 6; 62:7; 4 Ezra 13:25, 26). He will come to put down the mighty from their seats, to dethrone the kings of the earth, and to break the teeth of sinners (*Enoch* 42:2–6; 48:2–9; 62:5–9; 69:26–29). In apocalyptic there was nothing human or gentle about the Messiah; he was a divine figure of avenging power and glory before whom the earth trembled in terror.

(ii) The coming of the Messiah was to be preceded by the return of Elijah who would prepare the way for him (Malachi 4:5, 6). Elijah was to stand upon the hills of Israel, so the rabbis said, and announce the coming of the Messiah with a voice so great that it would sound from one end of the earth to the other.

(iii) The last terrible times were known as "the travail of the Messiah." The coming of the Messianic age would be like the agony of birth. In the Gospels Jesus is depicted as foretelling the signs of the end and is reported as saying: "All these things are the beginnings of sorrows" (Matthew 24:8; Mark 13:8). The word for *sorrow* is *odinai,* and it literally means *birthpangs.*

(iv) The last days will be a time of terror. Even the mighty men will cry bitterly (Zephaniah 1:14); the inhabitants of the land shall tremble (Joel 2:1); men will be affrighted with fear and all will seek some place to hide and will find none (*Enoch* 102:1, 3).

(v) The last days will be a time when the world will be shattered, a time of cosmic upheaval when the universe, as men know it, will be disintegrated. The stars will be extinguished; the sun will be turned into darkness and the moon into blood (Isaiah 13:10; Joel 2:30, 31; 3:1). The firmament will crash in ruins; there will be a cataract of raging fire, and creation will become a molten mass (*Sibylline Oracles* 3:83–89). The seasons will lose their order, and there will be neither night or dawn (*Sibylline Oracles* 3:796–806).

(vi) The last days will be a time when human relationships will be destroyed. Hatred and enmity will reign upon the earth. Every man's hand will be against his neighbour (Zechariah 14:13). Brothers will kill each other; parents will murder their own children; from dawn to sunset they shall slay one another (*Enoch* 100:1, 2). Honour will be turned into shame, and strength into humiliation, and beauty into ugliness. The man of humility will become the man of envy; and passion will hold sway over the man who once was peaceful (2 *Baruch* 48:31–37).

(vii) The last days will be a time of judgment. God will come like a refiner's fire, and who can endure the day of his coming (Malachi 3:1–3)? It is by the fire and the sword that God will plead with men (Isaiah 66:1,16). The Son of Man will destroy sinners from the earth (*Enoch* 69:27), and the smell of brimstone will pervade all things (*Sibylline Oracles* 3:58–61). The sinners will be burned up as Sodom was long ago (*Jubilees* 36;10, 11).

(viii) In all these visions the Gentiles have their place, but it is not always the same place.

(*a*) Sometimes the vision is that the Gentiles will be totally destroyed. Babylon will become such a desolation that there will be no place for the wandering Arab to plant his tent among the ruins, no place for the shepherd to graze his sheep; it will be nothing more than a desert inhabited by the beasts (Isaiah 13:19–22). God will tread down the Gentiles in his anger (Isaiah 63:6). The Gentiles will come over in chains to Israel (Isaiah 45:14).

(*b*) Sometimes there is depicted one last gathering of the Gentiles against Jerusalem, and one last battle in which they are destroyed (Ezekiel 38:14–39:16; Zechariah 14:1–11). The kings of the nations will throw themselves against Jerusalem; they will seek to ravage the shrine of the Holy One; they will place their thrones in a ring round the city, with their infidel people with them; but it will be only for their final destruction (*Sibylline Oracles* 3:663–672).

(*c*) Sometimes there is the picture of the conversion of the Gentiles through Israel. God has given Israel for a light to the Gentiles, that she may be God's salvation to the ends of the earth (Isaiah 49:6). The isles wait upon God (Isaiah 51:5); the ends of the earth are invited to look to God and be saved (Isaiah 45:20–22). The Son of Man will be a light to the Gentiles (*Enoch* 48:4, 5). Nations shall come from the ends of the earth to Jerusalem to see the glory of God (*Psalms of Solomon* 17:34).

Of all the pictures in connection with the Gentiles the commonest is that of the destruction of the Gentiles and the exaltation of Israel.

(ix) In the last days the Jews who have been scattered throughout the earth will be ingathered to the Holy City again. They will come back from Assyria and from Egypt and will worship the Lord in his holy mountain (Isaiah 27:12, 13). The hills will be removed and the valleys will be filled in, and even the trees will gather to give them shade, as they come back (Baruch 5:5–9). Even those who died as exiles in far countries will be brought back.

(x) In the last days the New Jerusalem, which is already prepared in heaven with God (4 Ezra 10:44–59; *2 Baruch* 4:2–6), will come down among men. It will be beautiful beyond compare with foundations of sapphires, and pinnacles of agate, and gates of carbuncles, on borders of pleasant stones (Isaiah 54:12, 13; Tobit 13:16, 17). The glory of the latter house will be greater than the glory of the former (Haggai 2:7–9).

(xi) An essential part of the apocalyptic picture of the last days was the resurrection of the dead. "Many of those who sleep in the dust of the earth shall awake, some to everlasting life, and some to shame and everlasting contempt" (Daniel 12:2, 3). Sheol and the grave will give back that which has been entrusted to them (*Enoch* 51:1). The scope of the resurrection of the dead varied. Sometimes it was to apply only to the righteous in Israel; sometimes to all Israel; and sometimes to all men everywhere. Whichever form it took, it is true to say that now for the first time we see emerging a strong hope of a life beyond the grave.

(xii) There were differences as to how long the Messianic kingdom was to last. The most natural—and the most usual—view was to think of it as lasting for ever. The kingdom of the saints is an everlasting kingdom (Daniel 7:27). Some believed that the reign of the Messiah would last for four hundred years. They arrived at this figure from a comparison of Genesis 15:13 and Psalm 90:15. In Genesis Abraham is told that the period of affliction of the children of Israel will be four hundred years; the psalmist's prayer is that God will make the nation glad according to the days wherein he has afflicted them and the years wherein they have seen evil. In the Revelation the view is that there is to be a reign of the saints for a thousand years; then the final battle with the assembled powers of evil; then the golden age of God.

Such were the events which the apocalyptic writers pictured in the last days; and practically all of them find their place in the pictures of the Revelation. To complete the picture we may briefly summarize the blessings of the coming age.

4. The Blessings of the Age to Come

(i) The divided kingdom will be united again. The house of Judah will walk again with the house of Israel (Jeremiah 3:18; Isaiah 11:13; Hosea 1:11). The old divisions will be healed and the people of God will be one.

(ii) There will be in the world an amazing fertility. The wilderness will become a field (Isaiah 32:15); it will become like the garden of Eden (Isaiah 51:3); the desert will rejoice and blossom like the crocus (Isaiah 35:1). The earth will yield its fruit ten thousandfold; on each vine will be a thousand branches, on each branch a thousand cluster, in each cluster a thousand grapes, and each grape will give a cor (120 gallons) of wine (*2 Baruch* 29:5–8). There will be a plenty such as the world has never known and the hungry will rejoice.

(iii) A consistent part of the dream of the new age was that in it all wars would cease. The swords will be beaten into ploughshares and the spears into pruning-hooks (Isaiah 2:4). There will be no sword or battle-din. There will be a common law for all men and a great peace throughout the earth, and king will be friendly with king (*Sibylline Oracles* 3:751–760).

(iv) One of the loveliest ideas concerning the new age was that in it there would be no more enmity between the beasts or between man and the beasts. The leopard and the kid, the cow and the bear, the lion and the fatling will play and lie down together (Isaiah 11:6–9; 65:25). There will be a new covenant between man and the beasts of the field (Hosea 2:18). Even a child will be able to play where the poisonous reptiles have their holes and their dens (Isaiah 11:6–9; *2 Baruch* 73:6). In all nature there will be a universal reign of friendship in which none will wish to do another any harm.

(v) The coming age will bring the end of weariness, of sorrow and of pain. The people will not sorrow any more (Jeremiah 31:12); everlasting joy will be upon their heads (Isaiah 35:10). There will be no such thing as an untimely death (Isaiah 65:20–22); no man will say: "I am sick" (Isaiah 33:24); death will be swallowed up in victory and God will wipe tears from all faces (Isaiah 25:8). Disease will withdraw; anxiety, anguish and lamentation will pass away; childbirth will have no pain; the reaper will not grow weary and the builder will not be toilworn (*2 Baruch* 73:2–74:4). The age to come will be one when what Virgil called "the tears of things" will be no more.

(vi) The age to come will be an age of righteousness. There will be perfect holiness among men. Mankind will be a good generation, living in the fear of the Lord in the days of mercy (*Psalms of Solomon* 17:28–49; 18:9, 10).

The Revelation is the New Testament representative of all these apocalyptic works which tell of the terrors before the end of time and of the blessings of the age to come; and it uses all the familiar imagery. It may often be difficult and even unintelligible to us, but for the most part it was using pictures and ideas which those who read it would know and understand.

CHAPTER THIRTY-FIVE

The Means of God's Revelation

Revelation 1:1–3

Let us note the *content* of the revelation which comes to John. It is the revelation of "the things which *must quickly* happen" (1:1). There are two important words here. There is *must*. History is not haphazard; it has purpose. There is *quickly*. Here is the proof that it is quite wrong to use the Revelation as a kind of mysterious timetable of what is going to happen thousands of years from now. As John sees it, the things it deals with are working themselves out immediately. The Revelation must be interpreted against the background of its own time.

The man who keeps these words is blessed. To hear God's word is a privilege; to obey it is a duty. There is no real Christianity in the man who hears and forgets or deliberately disregards.

That is all the more true because the time is short. The time is near (verse 3). The early church lived in vivid expectation of the coming of Jesus Christ and that expectation was "the ground of hope in distress and constant heed to warning." Apart altogether from that, no man knows when the call will come to take him from this earth, and in order to meet God with confidence he must add the obedience of his life to the listening of his ear.

CHAPTER THIRTY-SIX

The Coming Glory

Revelation 1:7

From now on in almost every passage, we shall have to note John's continuous use of the Old Testament. He was so soaked in the Old Testament that it was almost impossible for him to write a paragraph without quoting it. This is interesting and significant. John was living in a time when to be a Christian was an agonizing thing. He himself knew banishment and imprisonment and hard labour; and there were many who knew death in its most cruel forms. The best way to maintain courage and hope in such a situation was to remember that God had never failed in the past; and that his power was not grown less now.

In this passage John sets down the motto and the text of his whole book, his confidence in the triumphant return of Christ, which would rescue Christians in distress from the cruelty of their enemies.

(i) To Christians the return of Christ is a *promise on which to feed the soul.* John takes as his picture of that return Daniel's vision of the four bestial powers who have held the world in their grip (Daniel 7:1–14). There was Babylon, the power that was like a lion with eagle's wings (7:4). There was Persia, the power that was like a savage bear (7:5). There was Greece, the power that was like a winged leopard (7:6). There was Rome, a beast with iron teeth, beyond description (7:7). But the day of these bestial empires was over, and the dominion was to be given to a gentle power like a son of man. "I saw in the night visions, and, behold, with the clouds of heaven there came one like a son of man, and he came to the Ancient of Days, and was presented before him, and to him was given dominion, and glory, and kingdom, that all peoples, nations and languages should serve him" (7:13, 14). It is from that passage in Daniel there emerges the ever-recurring picture of the Son of Man coming on the clouds (Mark 13:26; 14:62; Matthew 24:30; 26:64). When we strip away the purely temporary imagery—we, for instance, no longer think of heaven as a localized place above the sky—we are left with the unchanging truth that the day will come when Jesus Christ will be Lord of all. In that hope have ever been the strength and the comfort of Christians for whom life was difficult and for whom faith meant death.

(ii) To the enemies of Christ, *the return of Christ is a threat.* To make this point John again quotes the Old Testament, from Zechariah 12:10 which contains the words: "When they look on him whom they have pierced, they shall mourn for him, as one mourns for an only child, and weep bitterly over him, as one weeps over a first-born." The story behind the Zechariah saying is this. God gave his people a good shepherd; but the people in their disobedient folly killed him and took to themselves evil and self-seeking shepherds. But the day will come when in the grace of God they will bitterly repent, and in that day they will look on the good shepherd whom they pierced and will sorrowfully lament for him and for what they have done. John takes that picture and applies it to Jesus. Men crucified him but the day will come when they will look on him again; and this time, he will not be a broken figure on a cross but a regal figure to whom universal dominion has been given.

The first reference of these words is to the Jews and the Romans who actually crucified Jesus. But in every age all who sin crucify him again. The day will come when those who disregarded and those who opposed Jesus Christ will find him the Lord of the universe and the judge of their souls.

The passage closes with the two exclamations—"Even so. Amen!" In the Greek the words are *nai* and *amen. Nai* is the Greek and *amen* is the Hebrew for a solemn affirmation—"Yes, indeed! So let it be!" By using the expression both in Greek and Hebrew John underlines its awful solemnity.

CHAPTER THIRTY-SEVEN

The Black Horse of Famine

Revelation 6:5–6

It will help us to understand the idea behind this passage if we remember that John is giving an account not of the end of things, but of the signs and events which precede the end. So here the black horse and its rider represent famine, a famine which is very severe and causes great hardship, but which is not desperate enough to kill. There is wheat—at a prohibitive price; and the wine and the oil are not affected.

A measure of wheat or three measures of barley was to cost a *denarius*. The measure was a *choinix*, equivalent to two pints and consistently defined in the ancient world as a man's ration for a day. A *denarius* was the equivalent of four pence and was a working man's wage for a day. Normally one *denarius* bought anything from eight to sixteen measures of corn and three to four times as much barley. What John is foretelling is a situation in which a man's whole working wage would be needed to buy enough corn for himself for a day, leaving absolutely nothing to buy any of the other necessities of life and absolutely nothing for his wife and family. If instead of corn he bought the much inferior barley, he might manage to give some to his wife and family but again he would have nothing to buy anything else.

We have seen that, although John was telling of the signs which were to precede the end, he was nevertheless painting them in terms of actual historical situations which men would recognize. This passage finds an amazing echo in certain events during the reign of Domitian, at the very time when John was writing. There was a very serious shortage of grain and also a superabundance of wine. Domitian took the drastic step of enacting that no fresh vine-yards should be planted and that half the vineyards in the provinces should be cut down. At this edict the people of the province of Asia, in which John was writing, came very near to rebelling for their vine-yards were one of their principal sources of revenue. In view of the violent reaction of the people of Asia, Domitian rescinded his edict and actually enacted that those who allowed their vineyards to go out of cultivation should be prosecuted. Here is the very picture of a situation in which corn was scarce and it was yet forbidden to interfere with the supply of wine and oil.

So, then, this is a picture of famine set alongside luxury. There is always something radically wrong with a situation in which some have too much and others too little. This is always a sign that the society in which it occurs is hastening to its ruin.

CHAPTER THIRTY-EIGHT

The Pale Horse of
Pestilence and Death

Revelation 6:7–8

As we approach this passage we must once again remember that it is telling not of the final end but of the signs which precede it. That is why it is a fourth part of the earth which is involved in death and disaster. This is a terrible time but it is not the time of total destruction.

The picture is a grim one. The horse is *pale* in colour. The word is *chloros* which means pale in the sense of livid and is used of a face blanched with terror. The passage is complicated by the fact that the Greek word *thanatos* is used in a double sense. In verse 8 it is used to mean both *death* and *pestilence.*

John was writing in a time when famine and pestilence did devastate the world; but in this case he is thinking in terms provided by the Old Testament which more than once speaks of "the four sore judgments." Ezekiel hears God tell of the time when he will send his "four sore acts of judgment upon Jerusalem"—sword, famine, evil beasts, and pestilence (Ezekiel 14:21). In Leviticus there is a passage which tells of the penalties which God will send upon his people because of their disobedience. Wild beasts will rob them of their children and destroy their cattle and make them few in number. The sword will avenge their breaches of the covenant. When they are gathered in their cities the pestilence will be among them. He will break the staff of bread and they will eat and not be satisfied (Leviticus 26:21–26).

Here John is using a traditional picture of what is to happen when

God despatches his wrath upon his disobedient people. At the back of it all is the permanent truth that no man or nation can escape the consequences of their sin.

CHAPTER THIRTY-NINE

The Shattered Universe

Revelation 6:12–14

John is using pictures very familiar to his Jewish readers. The Jews always regarded the end as a time when the earth would be shattered and there would be cosmic upheaval and destruction. In the picture there are, as it were, five elements which can all be abundantly illustrated from the Old Testament and from the books written between the Testaments.

(i) There is the *earthquake*. At the coming of the Lord the earth will tremble (Amos 8:8). There will be a great shaking in the land of Israel (Ezekiel 38:19). The earth will quake and the heavens will tremble (Joel 2:10). God will shake the heavens and the earth and the sea and the dry land (Haggai 2:6). The earth will tremble and be shaken to its bounds; the hills will be shaken and fall (*Assumption of Moses* 10:4). The earth shall open and fire burst forth (2 Esdras 5:8). Whoever gets out of the war will die in the earthquake; and whoever gets out of the earthquake will die in the fire, and whoever gets out of the fire will perish in the famine (*2 Baruch* 70:8). The Jewish prophets and seers saw a time when earth would be shattered and a tide of destruction would flow over the old world before the new world was born.

(ii) There is *the darkening of the sun and moon.* The sun will set at midday, and earth will grow dark in the clear daylight (Amos 8:9). The stars will not shine; the sun will be darkened in his going forth and the moon will not cause her light to shine (Isaiah 13:10). God will clothe the heavens with blackness and will make sackcloth their covering (Isaiah 50:3). God will make the stars dark and cover the sun with a cloud (Ezekiel 32:7). The sun will be turned into darkness and the moon into blood (Joel 2:31). The horns of the sun will be broken and he will be turned into darkness, the moon will not give her light, and will be turned into blood; and the circle of the stars will be disturbed (*Assumption of Moses* 10:4, 5). The sun will be darkened and the moon will not give her light (Matthew 24:29; Mark 13:24; Luke 23:45).

(iii) There is *the falling of the stars.* To the Jew this idea was specially terrible, for the order of the heavens was the very guarantee of the unchanging fidelity of God. Take away the reliability of the heavens and there was nothing left but chaos. The angel tells Enoch to behold the heavens, to see how the heavenly bodies never change their orbits or transgress against their appointed order (*Enoch* 2:1). Enoch saw the chambers of the sun and moon, how they go out and come in, how they never leave their orbit, and add nothing to it and take nothing from it (*Enoch* 41:5). To the Jew the last word in chaos was a world of falling stars. But in the end time the host of heaven would be dissolved and fall down as the leaf falls from the vine and the fig from the fig tree (Isaiah 34:4). The stars will fall from heaven and the powers of heaven shall be shaken (Matthew 24:29). The firmament shall fall on the sea and a cataract of fire will reduce the heavens and the stars to a molten mass (*Sibylline Oracles* 3:83). The stars will transgress their order and alter their orbits (*Enoch* 80:5, 6). The outgoings of the stars will change (2 Esdras 5:4). The end will be a time when the most reliable things in the universe will become a disorderly and terrifying chaos.

(iv) There is *the folding up of the heavens.* The picture in this passage is of a roll stretched out and held open, and then suddenly split down the middle so that each half recoils and rolls up. God will shake the heavens (Isaiah 13:13). The heavens will be rolled together as a scroll (Isaiah 34:4). They will be changed like a garment and folded up (Psalm 102:25, 26). At the end the eternal heavens themselves will be rent in two.

(v) There is *the moving of the hills and of the islands of the sea.* The mountains will tremble and the hills will be moved (Jeremiah 4:24). The mountains will quake and the hills will melt (Nahum 1:5). John saw a time when the most unshakeable things would be shaken and when even rocky isles like Patmos would be lifted from their foundation.

Strange as John's pictures may seem to us, there is not a single detail which is not in the pictures of the end time in the Old Testament and in the books written between the Testaments. We must not think that these pictures are to be taken literally. Their point is that John is taking every terrifying thing that can be imagined and piling them all together to give a picture of the terrors of the end time. Today, with our increased scientific knowledge, we might well paint the picture in different terms; but it is not the picture that matters. What matters is the terrors which John and the Jewish seers foresaw when God would invade the earth when time was coming to an end.

CHAPTER FORTY

Rescue and Reward

Revelation 7:1–3

John is seeing the vision of the last terrible days and in particular the great tribulation which is to come, such as was not since the beginning of the world to this time (Matthew 24:21; Mark 13:19). In this coming tribulation there was to be a final assault by every evil power and a final devastation of the earth. It is to play their part in this devastation that the winds are waiting and from which for a little while they are being held in check.

Before this time of terror and devastation comes, the faithful are to be sealed with the seal of God in order that they may survive it. It is not that they are to be exempt from it but that they are to be brought safely through it.

This is a terrible picture; even if the faithful are to be brought through this terrible time, they none the less must pass through it, and this is a prospect to make even the bravest shudder.

In verse 9 the range of the seer's vision extends still further and he sees the faithful after the tribulation has passed. They are in perfect peace and satisfaction in the very presence of God. The last time will bring them unspeakable horrors, but when they have passed through it they will enter into equally unspeakable joy.

There are really three elements in this picture. (i) There is a *warning*. The last unparalleled and inconceivable time of tribulation is coming soon. (ii) There is an *assurance*. In that time of destruction the faithful will suffer terribly, but they will come out on the other side because they are sealed with the seal of God. (iii) There is a *promise*.

When they have passed through that time, they will come to the blessedness in which all pain and sorrow are gone and there is nothing but peace and joy.

CHAPTER FORTY-ONE

The Seal of God

Revelation 7:4–8

Those who are to be brought safely through the great tribulation are sealed upon their foreheads. The origin of this picture is very likely in Ezekiel 9. In Ezekiel's picture, before the final slaughter begins, the man with the inkhorn marks the forehead of those who are faithful and the avengers are told that none so marked must be touched (Ezekiel 9:1–7).

Very commonly a seal indicated source or possession. A merchant would seal a package of goods to certify that it belonged to him; and the owner of a vineyard would seal jars of wine to show that they came from his vineyard and with his guarantee.

So here the seal was a sign that these people belonged to God and were under his power and authority.

In the early church this picture of sealing was specially connected with two things. (*a*) It was connected with baptism which was regularly described as sealing. It is as if, when a person was baptized, a mark was put upon him to show that he had become the property and the possession of God. (*b*) Paul regularly talks about the Christian being sealed with the gift of the Holy Spirit. The possession of the Holy Spirit is the sign that a man belongs to God. The real Christian is marked out by the seal of the Spirit which enables him to have the wisdom and the strength to cope with life in a way beyond the attainment of others.

There are certain quite general things to be noted here which will greatly help towards the interpretation of this passage.

(i) Two things are to be said about the number 144,000. (*a*) It is quite certain that it does not stand for the number of the faithful in every day and generation. The 144,000 stands for those who in the time of John are sealed and preserved from the great tribulation which at that moment was coming upon them. In due time, as we see in verse 9, they are to be merged with the great crowd beyond all counting and drawn from every nation. (*b*) The number 144,000 stands, not for limitation, but for completeness and perfection. It is made up of 12 multiplied by 12—the perfect square—and then rendered even more inclusive and complete by being multiplied by 1,000. This does not tell us that the number of the saved will be very small; it tells us that the number of the saved will be very great.

(ii) The enumeration in terms of the twelve tribes of Israel does not mean that this is to be read in purely Jewish terms. One of the basic thoughts of the New Testament is that the church is the real Israel, and that the national Israel has lost all its privileges and promises to the church. Paul writes: "He is not a real Jew who is one outwardly, nor is true circumcision something external and physical. He is a Jew who is one inwardly, and real circumcision is a matter of the heart, spiritual and not literal. His praise is not from men but from God" (Romans 2:28, 29). "Not all who are descended from Israel belong to Israel," says Paul (Romans 9:6, 7). If a man is Christ's, then is he Abraham's seed and an heir according to the promise (Galatians 3:29). It is the church which is the Israel of God (Galatians 6:16). It is Christians who are the real circumcision, those who worship God in the spirit, who rejoice in Christ Jesus and who have no confidence in the flesh (Philippians 3:3). Even if this passage is stated in terms of the twelve tribes of Israel, the reference is still to the church of God, the new Israel, the Israel of God.

(iii) It would be a mistake to place any stress on the order in which the twelve tribes are given, because the lists of the tribes are always varying in their order. But two things stand out. (*a*) Judah comes first, thus supplanting Reuben, who was the eldest son of Jacob. That is simply explained by the fact it was from the tribe of Judah that the Messiah came. (*b*) Much more interesting is the omission of Dan. But there is also an explanation of that. In the Old Testament Dan does not hold a high place and is often connected with idolatry. In Jacob's dying speech to his sons, it is said: "Dan shall be a serpent in the way, a viper by the path, that bites the horse's heels, so that his rider falls backward" (Genesis 49:17). In Judges the children of Dan are said to have set up a graven image (Judges 18:30). The golden calves, which became a sin, were set up in Bethel and in Dan (1 Kings 12:29). There is more. There is a curious saying in Jeremiah 8:16: "The snorting of their horses is heard from Dan; at the sound of the neighing of their stallions the whole land quakes. They come and devour the land and all that fills it." That saying came to be taken as referring to Antichrist, the coming incarnation of evil; and it came to be believed among the Jewish rabbis that Antichrist was to spring from Dan. Hippolytus (*Concerning Antichrist* 14) says: "As the Christ was born from the tribe of Judah, so will the Antichrist be born from the tribe of Dan." That is why Dan is missed out from this list and the list completed by the including of Manasseh, who is normally included in Joseph.

CHAPTER FORTY-TWO

Unlocking the Abyss

Revelation 9:1–2

The picture of terror mounts in its awful intensity. Now the terrors coming upon the earth are beyond nature; they are demonic; the abyss is being opened and superhuman terrors are being despatched upon the world.

The picture will become clearer if we remember that John thinks of the stars as living beings. This is common in *Enoch* where, for instance, we read of wandering and disobedient stars being bound hand and foot and cast into the abyss (*Enoch* 86:1; 88:1). To the Jewish mind the stars were divine beings, who by disobedience could become demonic and evil.

In the Revelation we read fairly often of the *abyss* or the *bottomless pit*. The abyss is the intermediate place of punishment of the fallen angels, the demons, the beast, the false prophet and of Satan (9:1, 2, 11; 11:7; 20:1, 3). Their final place of punishment is the lake of burning fire and brimstone (20:10, 14, 15). To complete the picture of these terrors we may add that Gehenna—which is not mentioned in the Revelation—is the place of punishment for evil men.

This idea of the abyss underwent a development. In the beginning it was the place of the imprisoned waters. In the creation story the primaeval waters surround the earth and God separates them by creating the firmament (Genesis 1:6,7). In its first idea the abyss was the place where the flood of the waters was confined by God beneath the earth, a kind of great subterranean sea, where the waters were imprisoned to make way for the dry land. The second step was that the abyss became the abode of the enemies of God, although even there they were not beyond his power and control (Amos 9:3; Isaiah 51:9; Psalm 74:13).

Next the abyss came to be thought of as a great chasm in the earth. We see this idea in Isaiah 24:21, 22, where the disobedient hosts of heaven and the kings of the earth are gathered together as prisoners in the pit.

This is the kind of picture in which inevitably horror mounts upon horror. The most detailed descriptions of the abyss are in *Enoch,* which was so influential between the Testaments. There it is the prison abode of the angels who fell, the angels who came to earth and seduced mortal women, the angels who taught men to worship demons instead of the true God (Genesis 6:1–4). There are grim descriptions of it. It has no firmament above and no firm earth beneath; it has no water; it has no birds; it is a waste and horrible place, the end of heaven and earth (*Enoch* 18:12–16). It is chaotic. There is a fire which blazes and a cleft into the abyss whose magnitude passes all conjecture (*Enoch* 21:1–10).

These things are not to be taken literally. The point is that in this terrible time of devastation which the seer sees coming upon the earth, the terrors are not natural but demonic; the powers of evil are being given their last chance to work their dreadful work.

CHAPTER FORTY-THREE

Things to Come

Revelation 11:14–19

What makes this passage difficult is that it seems to indicate that things have come to an end in final victory, while there is still half the book to go. The explanation, as we have seen, is that this passage is a summary of what is still to come. The events foreshadowed here are as follows.

(i) There is the victory in which the kingdoms of the world become the kingdoms of the Lord and of his Anointed One. This is really a quotation of Psalm 2:2, and is another way of saying that the Messianic reign has begun. In view of this victory the twenty-four elders, that is, the whole church, break out in thanksgiving.

(ii) This victory leads to the time when God takes his supreme authority (verse 17). That is to say, it leads to the thousand year reign of God, the Millennium, a thousand year period of peace and prosperity.

(iii) At the end of the Millennium there is to come the final attack of all the hostile powers (verse 18); they will be finally defeated and then will follow the last judgment.

In verse 19 we come back, as it were, to the present. There is a vision of the heavenly Temple opened and of the Ark of the Covenant. Two things are involved in this vision.

(i) The Ark of the Covenant was in the Holy of Holies, the inside of which no ordinary person had ever seen, and into which even the High Priest went only on the Day of Atonement. This must mean that now the glory of God is going to be fully displayed.

(ii) The reference to the Ark of the Covenant is as a reminder of

God's special covenant with his people. Originally that covenant had been with the people of Israel; but the new covenant is with all of every nation who love and believe in Jesus. Whatever the terror to come, God will not be false to his promises.

This is a picture of the coming of the full glory of God, a terrifying threat to his enemies but an uplifting promise to the people of his covenant.

CHAPTER FORTY-FOUR

The Power of the Beast
Revelation 13

It will be much easier if we treat this chapter as a whole before we undertake any detailed study of it. That is all the more necessary because this chapter is the essence of the whole book.

The general meaning is this. Satan, cast out of heaven, knows that his time is short and is determined to do as much damage as he can. To cause that damage on earth he delegates his power to the two beasts who are the central figures in this chapter.

The beast from the sea stands for the Roman Empire, to John the incarnation of evil, and is described in terms which come from Daniel. In Daniel 7:3–7 there is a vision of four great beasts who come out of the sea; they are the symbols of the great empires which have held world power and of an empire which, when Daniel was written, was holding world sway. The beast like a lion with an eagle's wings stands for Babylon; the one like a bear stands for Media; the one like a leopard with four wings stands for Persia; and the fourth stands for the empire of Alexander the Great. As the writer of Daniel saw these world powers, they were so savage and inhuman that they could be symbolized by nothing but bestial figures. It was only natural for a Jew to go back to this picture of the beastly empires when he wished to find a picture of another satanic empire threatening God's people in his own day.

John's picture in the Revelation puts together in the one beast the features of all four. It is like a leopard with bear's feet and a lion's mouth. That is to say, for John the Roman Empire was so satanic that it included all the terrors of the evil empires which had gone before.

This beast has *seven heads* and *ten horns.* These stand for the rulers and the emperors of Rome. Since Augustus, the first Roman Emperor, there had been seven emperors; Tiberius, A.D. 14–37; Caligula, A.D. 37–41; Claudius, A.D. 41–54; Nero, A.D. 55–68; Vespasian, A.D. 69–79; Titus, A.D. 79–81; Domitian, A.D. 81–96. These seven emperors are the seven heads of the beast. But in addition it is said that the beast had *ten* horns. The explanation of this second figure lies in this. After the death of Nero there was a short period of almost complete chaos. In eighteen months three different men briefly occupied the imperial power, Galba, Otho and Vitellius. They are not included in John's list of the seven heads but are included in the list of the ten horns.

John says that on the heads of the beast there were *blasphemous names.* These are the titles which the emperors took to themselves. Every emperor was called *divus* or *sebastos,* which means *divine.* Frequently the very name *God* or *Son of God* was given to the emperors; and Nero on his coins called himself *The Saviour of the World.* For any man to call himself divine was a blasphemous insult to God. Further, the later emperors took as their title the Latin word *dominus,* or its Greek equivalent *kurios,* both of which mean *lord* and in the Old Testament are the special title of God and in the New Testament the special title of Jesus Christ.

The second beast which figures in this chapter, the beast from the land, is the whole provincial organisation of magistrates and priesthoods designed to enforce Caesar worship, which confronted the Christians with the choice either of saying, "Caesar is Lord," or of dying.

So, then, our picture falls into place. These two savage beasts, the might of Rome and the organisation of Caesar worship, launched their combined attack on the Christians—and no nation had ever withstood the might of Rome. What hope had the Christians—poor, defenceless, outlaws?

There is another recurring theme in this chapter. Among the seven heads there is one which has been mortally wounded and restored to life (verse 3); that head above all is to be worshipped (verses 12 and 14); it is the supreme evil, the supreme enemy of Christ.

We have seen that the seven heads stand for the seven Roman emperors. A head wounded and restored to life will, therefore, stand for an emperor who died and came to life again. Here is symbolized the *Nero redivivus,* or Nero resurrected, legend which the Christians fused with the idea of Antichrist. In the *Sibylline Oracles* we read of the expectation in the last terrible days of the coming of a king from Babylon whom all men hate, a king fearful and shameless and of abominable parentage (5:143–148). A matricide shall come from the east and bring ruin on the world (5:361–364). One who dared the pollution of a mother's murder will come from the east (4:119–122). An exile from Rome with a myriad of swords shall come from beyond the Euphrates (4:137–139).

It is only when we realize what Nero was that we see how his return might well seem the coming of Antichrist.

No man ever started life with a worse heritage than Nero. His father was Cnaeus Domitius Ahenobarbus, who was notorious for wickedness. He had killed a freedman for no other crime than refusing to drink more wine; he had deliberately run over a child in his chariot on the Appian Way; in a brawl in the Forum he had gouged out the eye of a Roman knight; and he finally died of dropsy brought on by his debauchery. His mother was Agrippina, one of the most terrible women in history. When Ahenobarbus knew that he and Agrippina were to have a child he cynically said that nothing but a monstrous abomination could come from himself and her. When Nero was three, Agrippina was banished by the Emperor Caligula.

Under the Emperor Claudius, Agrippina was recalled from exile. She had now only one ambition—somehow to make her son emperor. She was warned by fortune-tellers that, if ever Nero became emperor, the result for her would be disaster. Her answer was: "Let him kill me, so long as he reigns."

Agrippina set to work with all the passion and the intrigue of her stormy nature. Claudius already had two children, Octavia and

Britannicus, but Agrippina badgered him into adopting Nero as his son, when Nero was eleven years of age, and persuaded him to marry her although he was her uncle. Steadily Britannicus, the heir to the throne, was pushed into the background and Nero was given the limelight.

For five years the marriage lasted and then Agrippina arranged for Claudius's poisoning by a dish of poisoned mushrooms. When Claudius lay in a coma, she hastened his end by brushing his throat with a poisoned feather. No sooner had Claudius died, than Nero was led forth as emperor, the army having been bribed to support him.

Then Nero embarked on a career of vicious crime. At night with other gilded youths he would roam the streets attacking all whom he could find. Worse was to come. He murdered Britannicus as a possible rival.

No young man or woman was safe from his lust. He was a blatant homosexual. He publicly married a youth named Sporus in a state wedding; and he took Sporus with him on a bridal tour of Greece. He was "married" to a freedman called Doryphorus. He took Poppaea Sabina, the wife of Otho, his closest friend, as his paramour, and kicked her to death when she was with child.

He had a passion for wild extravagance and extracted money from all and sundry. The imperial court was a welter of murder, immorality and crime.

One of Nero's passions was building. In A.D. 64 came the great fire of Rome which burned for a week. There is not the slightest doubt that Nero began it or that he hindered every attempt to extinguish it, so that he might have the glory of rebuilding the city. The people well knew who was responsible for the fire but Nero diverted the blame on to the Christians and the most deliberately sadistic of all persecutions broke out. He had the Christians sown up in the skins of wild animals and set his savage hunting dogs upon them. He had them enclosed in sacks with stones and flung into the Tiber. He had them coated with pitch and set alight as living torches to light the gardens of his palace.

The insanity of evil grew wilder and wilder. Anyone who incurred Nero's slightest displeasure was killed.

Agrippina made some attempt to control him and finally he turned against her. He made repeated attempts to murder her—by poison, by causing the roof of her house to collapse, by sending her to sea in a boat designed to break up. Finally, he sent his freedman Anicetus to stab her to death. When Agrippina saw the dagger, she bared her body. "Strike my womb," she said, "because it bore a Nero."

It could not last. First Julius Vindex rebelled in Gaul, then Galba in Spain. Finally the senate took its courage in its hands and declared Nero a public enemy. In the end he died by suicide in the wretched villa of a freedman called Phaon.

This is the head of the beast, wounded and restored; the Antichrist whom John expected was the resurrected Nero.

CHAPTER FORTY-FIVE

The Number of the Beast

Revelation 13:18

In this verse we are told that the number of the beast is six hundred and sixty-six. Who is this satanic beast so symbolized? It must be remembered that the ancient peoples had no figures and the letters of the alphabet did duty for numbers as well. This is as if in English we used A for 1, B for 2, C for 3, D for 4, and so on. Every word, therefore, and in particular every proper name, can also be a number. One charming and romantic way in which use was made of this fact is quoted by Deissmann. On the walls of Pompeii a lover wrote: "I love her whose number is 545," and thereby he at one and the same time identified and concealed his loved one!

The suggestions as to the meaning of 666 are endless. Since it is the number of the beast, everyone has twisted it to fit his own archenemy; and so 666 has been taken to mean the Pope, John Knox, Martin Luther, Napoleon and many another. Dr. Kepler provides us with an example of what ingenuity was produced during the Second World War. Let A = 100; B = 101; C = 102; D = 103 and so on. Then we can make this addition:

H = 107
I = 108
T = 119
L = 111
E = 104
R = 117

and the sum is 666!

Very early we saw that the Revelation is written in code; it is clear that nowhere will the code be more closely guarded than in regard to this number which stands for the arch-enemy of the church. The strange thing is that the key must have been lost very early; for even so great a Christian scholar as Irenaeus in the second century did not know what the number stood for.

The chapter itself gives us by far the best clue. There recurs again and again the mention of the head that was wounded to death and then restored. We have already seen that that head symbolizes the *Nero redivivus* legend. We might well, therefore, act on the assumption that the number has something to do with Nero. Many ancient manuscripts give the number as 616. If we take Nero in Latin and give it its numerical equivalent, we get:

N = 50
E = 6
R = 500
O = 60
N = 50

The total is 666; and the name can equally well be spelled without the final N which would give the number 616. In Hebrew the letters of Nero Caesar also add up to 666.

There is little doubt that the number of the beast stands for Nero; and that John is forecasting the coming of Antichrist in the form of Nero, the incarnation of all evil, returning to this world.

CHAPTER FORTY-SIX

The Harvest of Judgment

Revelation 14:14–20

The final vision of this chapter is of judgment depicted in pictures which were very familiar to Jewish thought.

It begins with the picture of the victorious figure of one like a son of man. This comes from Daniel 7:13, 14: "And I saw in the night visions, and, behold with the clouds of heaven, there came one like a son of man and he came to the ancient of days, and was presented before him. And to him was given dominion and glory and kingdom, that all peoples, nations and languages should serve him."

This picture goes on to depict judgment in two metaphors familiar to scripture.

It depicts judgment in terms of *harvesting*. When Joel wished to say that judgment was near, he said: "Put in the sickle, for the harvest is ripe" (Joel 3:13). "When the grain is ripe," said Jesus, "at once he puts in the sickle, because the harvest has come" (Mark 4:29); and in the parable of the wheat and the tares he uses the harvest as a picture of judgment (Matthew 13:24–30; 37–43).

It depicts judgment in terms of the winepress, which consisted of an upper and a lower trough connected by a channel. The troughs might be hollowed out in the rock or they might be built of brick. The grapes were put into the upper trough which was on a slightly higher level. They were then trampled with the feet and the juice flowed down the connecting channel into the lower trough. Often in the Old Testament, God's judgment is likened to the trampling of the grapes. "The Lord flouted all my mighty men in the midst of me . . .

the Lord has trodden as in a winepress the virgin daughter of Judah" (Lamentations 1:15). "I have trodden the winepress alone; and from the peoples no one was with me; I trod them in my anger, and trampled them in my wrath; their lifeblood is sprinkled upon my garments" (Isaiah 63:3).

Here, then, we have judgment depicted in the two familiar figures of the harvest and of the winepress. To this is added another familiar picture. The winepress is to be trodden outside the city, that is, Jerusalem. Both in the Old Testament and in the books between the Testaments there was a line of thought which held that the Gentiles would be brought to Jerusalem and judged there. Joel has a picture of all the nations gathered into the valley of Jehoshaphat and judged there (Joel 3:2, 12). Zechariah has a picture of a last attack of the Gentiles on Jerusalem and of their judgment there (Zechariah 14:1–4).

There are two difficult things in this passage. First, there is the fact that the one like a son of man reaps and also an angel reaps. We may regard the one like the son of man the risen and victorious Lord, reaping the harvest of his own people, while the angel with the sharp sickle reaps the harvest of those destined for judgment.

Second, it is said that the blood came up to the horses' bridles and spread for a distance of sixteen hundred stades or furlongs. No one has ever discovered a really satisfying explanation of this. The least unsatisfactory explanation is that sixteen hundred stades is almost exactly the length of Palestine from north to south; and this would mean that the tide of judgment would flow over and include the whole land. In that case the figure would symbolically describe the completeness of the judgment.

CHAPTER FORTY-SEVEN

The False Prophet

Revelation 16:13–16

Our next problem is to identify the false prophet. The dragon is identified as Satan (12:3, 9). The beast, the Roman Empire with its Caesar worship, has already appeared in 13:1. But this is the first time the false prophet has appeared upon the scene. Since he appears without any explanation, we must assume that John believes that the reader already has the key to his identity.

The false prophet was a figure whom God's people were well warned to expect both in the Old and in the New Testament. In the Old Testament men are forbidden to listen to the false prophet, however impressive his signs may be, and it is laid down that the punishment for the false prophet is death (Deuteronomy 13:1–5). It was part of the regular duty of the Sanhedrin to deal with the false prophet and to condemn him to death. The Christian church was warned that false Christs and false prophets would arise to seduce Christ's people (Mark 13:22). H. B. Swete says of these false prophets that the name covers a whole class—"magic-vendors, religious impostors, fanatics, whether deceivers or deceived, regarded as persons who falsely interpret the mind of God. True religion has no worse enemies and Satan no better allies."

The false prophet is mentioned here and in 19:20 and 20:10; if we place two passages together, we will find a clue to his identity. 19:20 tells us that in the end the false prophet was captured along with the beast and he is described as the person who worked miracles before the beast, and deceived those who had the mark of the beast and worshipped its image. In 13:13, 14 we have a description of the second beast, the beast from the land; it is said that this second beast does great wonders . . . and that he deceives those who dwell on the earth by means of those miracles which he was allowed to do in the presence of the beast. That is to say, the works of the false prophet and the works of the second beast are identical; so, then, the false prophet and the beast from the land are to be identified. We have already seen that that beast is to be identified with the provincial organisation for the enforcement of emperor worship. The false prophet, then, stands for the organization which seeks to make men worship the emperor and abandon the worship of Jesus Christ.

A man who tries to introduce the worship of other gods, who tries to make men compromise with the state or with the world, who tries to seduce other men from the exclusive worship of God, is always a false prophet.

CHAPTER FORTY-EIGHT

The Thousand-Year Reign of Christ

Revelation 20

Chapter 20 opens with the binding of the devil in the abyss for a period of a thousand years (20:1–3). There follows the resurrection of the martyrs to reign with Christ for a thousand years, although the rest of the dead are not yet resurrected (20:4–6). At the end of the thousand years Satan is again loosed for a brief space; there is final conflict with the enemies of Christ who are destroyed with fire from heaven while Satan is cast for ever into the lake of fire and brimstone (20:7–10). Then comes the general resurrection and the general judgment (20:11–14); and finally the description of the new heaven and the new earth to take the place of the things which have passed away (21:1–22, 5).

Since the great importance of this chapter is that it is what might be called the foundation document of Millenarianism or Chiliasm, it will be better to read it as a whole before we deal with it in detail.

Millennium means *a period of one thousand years;* and *chiliasm* is derived from the Greek *chilios, a thousand.* To put it briefly, the commonest form of Millenarianism teaches that for a thousand years before the end Christ will reign upon this earth in a kingdom of his saints; and after that will come the final struggle, the general resurrection, the last judgment and the final consummation.

We note two general facts. First, this was a very common belief in the early church and it still has its adherents. Second, this is the only passage in the New Testament in which it is clearly taught.

The picture is that first of all the Devil will be bound in the abyss for a thousand years. Then those who have been martyred for Christ and who have confessed his name before men will be resurrected, although the rest of mankind, even the Christians among them who did not suffer martyrdom, will not be resurrected. There will then be a period of a thousand years in which Christ and his saints will reign. After that for a brief time the Devil will be released. There will follow a final struggle and the general resurrection of all men. The devil will be finally defeated and cast into the lake of fire; his supporters will be burned up with fire from heaven; those whose names are in the Book of Life will enter into blessedness, but those whose names are not in the Book of Life will also be cast into the lake of fire.

This doctrine does not occur anywhere else in the New Testament but it was prevalent throughout the early church especially among those who had received their Christianity from Jewish sources. Here is our key. The origin of this doctrine is not specifically Christian but is to be found in certain Jewish beliefs about the Messianic age which were common in the time after 100 B.C.

Jewish Messianic beliefs were never an unvarying system. They varied from time to time and from thinker to thinker. The basis was that the Messiah would come and establish upon earth the new age, in which the Jewish nation would be supreme.

In the earlier times the general belief was that the kingdom so established would last for ever. God would set up a kingdom which would never be destroyed; it would break in pieces the other kingdoms, but it would stand for ever (Daniel 2:44). It was to be an everlasting dominion (Daniel 7:14, 27).

From 100 B.C. onwards there came a change. It was felt that this world was so incurably evil that within it the Kingdom of God could never finally come; and so there emerged the conception that the Messiah would have a limited reign and that after his reign the final consummation would come. The *Apocalypse of Baruch* foresees the defeat of the forces of evil; then the principate of the Messiah will stand for ever, until this world of corruption is at an end (*2 Baruch* 40:3). One section of *Enoch* sees history as a series of weeks. There are seven weeks of past history. The eighth is the week of the righteous, when a sword is given to the righteous and sinners are delivered into their hands, and the house of God is built. In the ninth week the evil are written down for destruction, and righteousness will flourish. In the tenth week comes judgment; and only then comes the eternal time of goodness and of God (*Enoch* 93:3–10).

There was much rabbinic discussion of how long the Messianic age would last before the final consummation arrived. Some said 40, some 100, some 600, some 1,000, some 2,000, some 7,000 years.

We look particularly at two answers. Second Esdras is very definite. God is represented as saying: "My Son the Messiah shall be revealed, together with those who are with him, and shall rejoice the survivors *for four hundred years*. And it shall be, after these years, that my Son the Messiah shall die, and all in whom there is human breath. Then shall the world be turned into the primaeval silence seven days, like as at the first beginnings, so that no man is left." And then after that the new age comes (2 Esdras 7:28, 29). This passage is unique in foretelling, not only a limited reign of the Messiah, but the Messiah's death. The period of four hundred years was arrived at by setting side by side two passages from the Old Testament. In Genesis 15:13 God tells Abraham that the period of the affliction of Israel will last for four hundred years. In Psalm 90:15 the prayer is: "Make us glad as many days as thou hast afflicted us, and as many years as we have seen evil." It was, therefore, held that the period of bliss, like the period of affliction, would last for 400 years.

More commonly it was held that the age of the world would correspond to the time taken for its creation and that the time of creation was 6,000 years. "A thousand years in thy sight are but as yesterday" (Psalm 90:4). "One day with the Lord is as a thousand years, and a thousand years as one day" (2 Peter 3:8). Each day of creation was said to be 1,000 years. It was, therefore, held that the Messiah would come in the sixth thousand of the years; and the seventh thousand, the equivalent of the Sabbath rest in the creation story, would be the reign of the Messiah.

Although the reign of the Messiah was to be the reign of righteousness, it was often conceived of in terms of material blessings.

"The earth also shall yield its fruit ten thousand-fold, and on each vine there shall be a thousand branches, and each branch shall produce a thousand clusters, and each cluster shall produce a thousand grapes, and each grape a cor (120 gallons) of wine" (*2 Baruch* 29:5, 6). There will be no more disease, no more untimely death; the beasts will be friendly with men; and women will have no pain in childbirth (*2 Baruch* 73).

Here, then, we have the background of the idea of the Millennium. Already the Jews had come to think of a limited reign of the Messiah, which would be a time of the triumph of righteousness, and of the greatest spiritual and material blessings.

On the basis of this passage of the Revelation Millenarianism or Chiliasm was very widespread within the early church, although it was never universal.

Millenarianism is by no means extinct within the church; but this is the only passage in the New Testament which unequivocally teaches it; its whole background is Jewish and not Christian, and the literal interpretation of it has always tended to run into danger and excess. It is a doctrine which has long since been left behind by the main stream of Christian thought and which now belongs to the eccentricities of Christian belief.

CHAPTER FORTY-NINE

The Chaining of Satan

Revelation 20:1–3

The abyss was a vast subterranean cavern beneath the earth, sometimes the place where all the dead went, sometimes the place where special sinners were kept awaiting punishment. It was reached by a chasm reaching down into the earth and this the angel locks in order to keep the Devil in the abyss.

It was the abyss which the devils feared most of all. In the story of the Gerasene demoniac the request of the devils was that Jesus would not command them to leave the man and to go out into the deep, that is, the abyss (Luke 8:31).

The seal is set on the chasm to ensure the safe-keeping of the prisoner, just as the seal was set on the tomb of Jesus to make sure that he would not escape (Matthew 27:66).

The Devil is to be kept in the abyss for a period of a thousand years. Even the way in which the word *thousand* is used in scripture warns us against taking this literally. Psalm 50:10 says that the cattle on a thousand hills belong to God; and Job 9:3 says that a man cannot answer God once in a thousand times. Thousand is simply used to describe a very large number.

At the end of the period the Devil is to be let loose for a little time. H. B. Swete suggests that the reason for the final loosing of the Devil is this. In a period of peace and righteousness, in a time when the opposition, so to speak, did not exist, it might easily happen that people came to take their faith unthinkingly. The loosing of the Devil meant a testing-time for Christians, and there are times when a testing-time is essential, if the reality of the faith is to be preserved.

CHAPTER FIFTY

The Privilege of Judgment

Revelation 20:4–5

In the first resurrection only those who have died and suffered for the faith are to be raised from the dead. The general resurrection is not to take place until after the thousand year reign of Christ upon earth. There is special privilege for those who have shown special loyalty to Christ.

Those who are to enjoy this privilege belong to two classes. First, there are those who have been martyred for their loyalty to Christ. The word used for the way in which they were killed means *to behead with an axe,* and denotes the most cruel death. Second, there are those who have not worshipped the beast and have not received his mark on their hand or on their forehead. H. B. Swete identifies these as those who, although they were not actually martyred, willingly bore suffering, reproach, imprisonment, loss of goods, disruption of their homes and personal relationships for the sake of Christ.

In the ancient church in the days of persecution two terms were used. *Martyrs* were those who actually died for their faith; *confessors* were those who suffered everything short of death for their loyalty to Christ. Both he who dies for Christ and he who lives for Christ will receive his reward.

Those who have been loyal to Christ are to receive the privilege of judgment. This is an idea which occurs more than once in the New Testament. Jesus is represented as saying that, when he returns to sit on the throne of his glory, his twelve apostles will sit on twelve thrones judging the twelve tribes of Israel (Matthew 19:28). Paul reminds the litigious Corinthians that the destiny of the saints is to judge the world (1 Corinthians 6:2). Again we do not need to take this literally. The idea symbolized is that the world to come will redress the balance of this one. In this world the Christian may be a man under the judgment of men; in the world to come the parts will be reversed and those who thought they were the judges will be the judged.

CHAPTER FIFTY-ONE

The Final Judgment

Revelation 20:11–15

Now comes the final judgment. God, the Judge, is on his great white throne which symbolizes his unapproachable purity.

It may be that some will find a problem here. The regular picture of the New Testament is that Jesus Christ is judge. John 5:22 represents Jesus as saying: "The Father judges no one, but has given all judgment to the Son." In the Parable of the Sheep and Goats it is the glorified Christ who is the judge (Matthew 25:31–46). In Paul's speech at Athens it is said that God has appointed a day in which he will judge the world by Jesus (Acts 17:31). In 2 Timothy 4:1 Jesus is the one who is about to judge the living and the dead.

There are two answers to this apparent difficulty.

First, the unity of the Father and the Son is such that there is no difficulty in ascribing the action of the one to the other. That is in fact what Paul does. In Romans 14:10 he writes: "We shall all stand before the judgment seat of God." But in 2 Corinthians 5:10 he writes: "We must all appear before the judgment seat of Christ."

Second, it may be that the real reason why God is the judge in John's Revelation is that the whole background of the book is Jewish; to a Jew, even when he became a Christian, God stood unique; and it would seem natural to him that God should be judge.

As John tells the story, the judgment begins with the passing away of this present world; earth and sky flee from his presence. John is thinking in pictures which are very familiar in the Old Testament. God laid the foundations of the earth, and the heavens are the work of his hands. Nonetheless it is still true that "they will perish . . . they will all wear out like a garment; thou changest them like raiment, and they pass away" (Psalm 102:25–27). "The heavens will vanish like smoke, the earth will wear out like a garment" (Isaiah 51:6). "Heaven and earth will pass away" (Mark 13:31). "The heavens will pass away with a loud noise, and the elements will be dissolved with fire, and the earth and the works that are upon it will be burned up" (2 Peter 3:10). The new man in Christ must have a new world in Christ.

Now follows the judgment of mankind.

It is the judgment of great and small. There is none so great as to escape the judgment of God, and none so unimportant as to fail to win his vindication.

Two kinds of books are mentioned. The first contains the records of the deeds of men. This is a common idea in scripture. "The court sat in judgment," says Daniel, "and the books were opened" (Daniel 7:10). In *Enoch* the sealed books are opened before the Lord of the sheep (*Enoch* 90:20). The *Apocalypse of Baruch* foretells the day when "the books shall be opened in which are written the sins of all those who have sinned, and again also the treasuries in which the righteousness of all those who have been righteous in creation is gathered" (2 *Baruch* 24:1). When the present age passes away, the books will be opened before the face of the firmament, and all shall see together (4 Ezra 6:20).

The idea is simply that a record of all men's deeds is kept by God. The symbolism is that all through life we are writing our own destiny; it is not so much that God judges a man as that a man writes his own judgment.

The second book is the Book of Life. This, too, occurs often in scripture. Moses is willing to be blotted out of the Book of Life if it will save the people (Exodus 32:32). It is the prayer of the Psalmist that the wicked will be blotted out of the Book of the Living and not written with the righteous (Psalm 69:28). Isaiah speaks of those who are written among the living (Isaiah 4:3). Paul speaks of his fellow labourers whose names are in the Book of Life (Philippians 4:3). It is the promise of the Risen Christ to the church at Sardis that the name of him who overcomes will not be blotted out of the Book of Life (Revelation 3:5). Those whose names are not written in the Book of Life are given over to destruction (Revelation 13:8). The idea behind this is that every ruler had a roll-book of living citizens under his control; and, of course, when a man died, his name was removed from the roll. Those whose names are in the Book of Life are those who are living, active citizens of the kingdom of God.

At the time of judgment it is said that the sea will give up its dead. The point is twofold. First, in the ancient world burial was all important; if a man did not obtain burial, his spirit would wander, homeless, neither in earth nor in heaven. And, of course, those who died at sea could never be buried. John means that even such as these will appear before the judgment seat of God. Second, H. B. Swete puts the matter in a more general form. "The accidents of death," he says, "will not prevent any from appearing before the judge." No matter how a man dies, he will not escape his punishment nor lose his reward.

Finally, Death and Hades are thrown into the lake of fire. As H. B. Swete puts it, these voracious monsters who have themselves devoured so many are in the end themselves destroyed. In the judgment those who are not in the Book of Life are condemned to the lake of fire with the Devil, their master, but for those whose names are in the Book of Life, death is for ever vanquished.

CHAPTER FIFTY-TWO

Last Words

Revelation 22:20–21

There is both pathos and glory in the way in which the Revelation ends. Amidst the terrible persecution of his day, the one thing which John longed for was the speedy return of Christ. That hope was never realized in the way in which he expected, but we can never doubt that Christ nevertheless abundantly kept his promise that he would be with his own even to the end of the world (Matthew 28:20).

Then comes the glory. Come what may, John was sure of the grace of the Lord Jesus Christ and equally sure that it was sufficient for all things.

It is surely symbolic, and it is surely fitting, that the last word of the Bible should be **GRACE.**

Topical Index of Passages